The Busy Manager's Guide to Successful Meetings

By
Karen Anderson

CAREER PRESS
180 Fifth Avenue
P.O. Box 34
Hawthorne, NJ 07507
1-800-CAREER-1
201-427-0229 (outside U.S.)
FAX: 201-427-2037

7-19-94

THE BUSY MANAGER'S GUIDE TO SUCCESSFUL MEETINGS
ISBN 1-56414-104-7, $16.95
Cover design by Digital Perspectives
Printed in the U.S.A. by Book-mart Press

To order this title by mail, please include price as noted above, $2.50
handling per order, and $1.00 for each book ordered. Send to: Career Press,
Inc., 180 Fifth Ave., P.O. Box 34, Hawthorne, NJ 07507

Or call toll-free 1-800-CAREER-1 (Canada: 201-427-0229) to order using
VISA or MasterCard, or for further information on books from Career Press.

Library of Congress Cataloging-in-Publication Data

Anderson, Karen, 1948-
    The busy manager's guide to successful meetings / by Karen
Anderson.
        p.   cm.
    ISBN 1-56414-104-7 : $16.95
    1. Meetings--Planning--Handbooks, manuals, etc. 2. Communication
in management--Handbooks, manuals, etc. I. Title.
HF5734.5.A53   1993
658.4'56--dc20
                                                              93-24811
                                                              CIP

Table of Contents

PREFACE

When I first saw this book, I thought, "A book on meetings? Sure. That sounds like something I'd really enjoy curling up with on a lazy Sunday afternoon." I've always considered meetings a necessary evil. I couldn't imagine myself willingly embracing the subject. But curiosity got the better of me, so I looked inside. I have to admit, I was pleasantly surprised. I was immediately struck by the simplicity of it, the usability, I guess you could say. There I was, a veteran of the meeting wars for longer than I care to remind myself, and I was finding little tricks that seemed so clever, so eminently usable. I found myself wishing I had a meeting to go to right then so I could try some of these things out.

The worst of it was I kept remembering all those endless, insufferable meetings I had endured in the past and thinking how easily that torment could have been avoided. It took me years of brutal experience to discover some of the most simple secrets this book exposes. I have to admit, I was impressed. I wish someone had put this book in my hands years ago. It would have spared me a lot of grief. But enough of that. Suffice it to say, any business person who has ever squandered even a few minutes of his or her valuable time in a useless meeting that dragged on and produced only ambiguous results at best will find this book compelling reading. It's packed with the kinds of little tricks that can really make a difference.

In short, if you hate meetings, you'll love this book.

***I*NTRODUCTION**

When both your mind and body go numb, when your ears refuse to listen a second longer and when your next yawn makes you realize you really are awake, but wish you weren't – that's when you know you're in another boring, endless meeting. Most meetings occur too often, last too long and accomplish too little.

Whether you attend meetings as a participant, an assistant or a leader, you have an investment in those meetings. Your investment may include your time, your presence, your preparation and your concentration. Your investment may also include your reputation – the skill with which you plan, conduct and contribute to meetings. This skill requires confidence and competence in multiple areas, such as organization, leadership, time management, space management, problem-solving, conflict resolution, oral and written communication, group dynamics and training strategies.

Gulp!

This list seems overwhelming, yet you already perform with reasonable confidence and competence in all these areas. Just consider how you manage a family and a home! Managing a household is a more complicated job than managing a meeting, but you don't think of it as anything exceptional. Yet, those skills are the same you'll use for running effective meetings, and running effective meetings is an exceptional skill. Your numb limbs and wide yawns in the last meeting attest to that!

You embark on an adventure each time you manage a meeting. Knowing how to save time, effort and money for your company by having fewer, shorter and better meetings is definitely to your career advantage. Check the following objectives and add any that you especially want to focus on while using this handbook.

OBJECTIVES:

▶ To save time by holding only necessary meetings

▶ To save time by starting and ending meetings at agreed times

▶ To save time by asking people to prepare or know background material prior to the meeting

▶ To save effort by preparing essential materials before any decisions must be made

▶ To save effort by including all essential decision makers in the meeting

▶ To save time and effort by communicating better the first time

▶ To save time and effort by encouraging team collaboration

▶ To save money by using company resources, such as personnel and property, as efficiently and effectively as possible

▶ To...

While pursuing those objectives, you'll experience some additional advantages. Check these and add any below that you especially want to develop.

ADVANTAGES:

▶ Increased self-awareness

▶ Increased self-confidence

▶ Increased visibility within your company

▶ Improved communications skills

▶ Improved leadership skills

▶ Improved organizational skills

▶ Increased or improved...

As you use this handbook, highlight tips you want to include in your repertoire of strategies and skills. Keep a personal index of comments and references on the Table of Contents page and concentrate on one chapter at a time. You will learn to manage meetings that occur just often enough, last just long enough and accomplish more than enough. The guidesheets, tips and examples included are practical, sequential steps to make planning meetings easy. The checklists at the end of each of the three parts of this handbook act as summaries and reminders to make your job easier. Let's begin.

Part I:
Preparation

"The readiness is all."
Hamlet

*C*HAPTER 1

Assessing Your Needs

How well you currently plan and run meetings will provide you with a point of reference. Use the **Self-Assessment Survey** on the following pages to identify your strengths and to establish your needs for improvement.

In this first chapter, you'll build a firm foundation for preparing your next meeting. Preparation includes assessing, planning, promoting, organizing and rehearsing both the context and the content of a meeting for a specific audience. Each of these steps is essential for assuring a successful meeting. Let's begin with assessing.

Self-Assessment Survey

Answer each item by checking the most representative column: Often, Sometimes or Seldom. Your honest answer is the "right answer."

	Often	Sometimes	Seldom
1. I schedule time on my daily calendar to prepare for a meeting.	[ ]	[ ]	[ ]
2. I plan only essential meetings whose purposes cannot be achieved in other ways.	[ ]	[ ]	[ ]
3. I set meeting objectives that are compatible with project goals and official company statements.	[ ]	[ ]	[ ]
4. I send both meeting announcements and agenda surveys to participants well in advance.	[ ]	[ ]	[ ]
5. I ask for attendance confirmation and/or make reminder memos or calls prior to the meeting day.	[ ]	[ ]	[ ]
6. I arrange documentation for the meeting in advance.	[ ]	[ ]	[ ]
7. I prepare materials needed for the meeting well in advance.	[ ]	[ ]	[ ]
8. I arrange for appropriate space for the meeting well in advance.	[ ]	[ ]	[ ]
9. I have a list of phone numbers for our support staff.	[ ]	[ ]	[ ]

continued

Self-Assessment Survey

	Often	Sometimes	Seldom
10. I ask participants to do something specific to prepare for the meeting, such as reading a report or bringing two quality-assurance ideas.	[ ]	[ ]	[ ]
11. I rehearse my presentation and test any media equipment well in advance.	[ ]	[ ]	[ ]
12. I analyze the audience's profile before the meeting.	[ ]	[ ]	[ ]
13. I use both visual and audio aids.	[ ]	[ ]	[ ]
14. I listen without interrupting.	[ ]	[ ]	[ ]
15. I practice conflict resolution and use these communication skills to run meetings smoothly.	[ ]	[ ]	[ ]
16. I involve participants within the first few minutes of a meeting.	[ ]	[ ]	[ ]
17. I am comfortable with a pause after a question in a meeting.	[ ]	[ ]	[ ]
18. I begin the next agenda at the end of this meeting.	[ ]	[ ]	[ ]
19. I make progress checks between meetings.	[ ]	[ ]	[ ]
20. I evaluate the process and my performance after each meeting.	[ ]	[ ]	[ ]

If you answered *Often* to 10 or more items in the **Self-Assessment Survey**, you are currently preparing for meetings better than your peers. If you answered *Sometimes* or *Seldom* five or more times, your meeting preparation needs tuning.

From this survey, you probably noticed how often tasks that ensure a successful meeting must be completed during the planning phase of the meeting. Preparation plays a key role in your effectiveness as a meeting leader. Preparing space, materials, topics, schedules, equipment and participants is too often neglected. Even more important is your attitude about the meeting.

Creating a welcome and warm atmosphere in which people can meet and work is crucial to the success of any meeting. Constructive meetings grow out of positive and productive interactions among members of your team. How you support each individual's efforts determines how well your meeting works. You want your family to enjoy and encourage each other at home. Similarly, you want your "family at work" to enjoy and encourage one another. This intent is your **HIDDEN Agenda**:

Honesty,

Integrity,

Dignity,

Development,

Empowerment and

Needs satisfaction.

> **In a recent survey of more than 2,000 business leaders, 87% said they make judgments about people's management ability based on how well they run meetings.**

Honesty

Most people rate **honesty** high on their list of personal values. Consider these statements made by adults in the workforce:

"All I want is to be treated fairly and honestly."

"I expect my boss and my peers to be truthful with me."

"Honesty is the only healthy policy."

"Trust is built on honest, open communication."

"Being honest is no excuse for being mean."

"Gentle honesty moves me farther faster than harsh honesty does."

"Building rapport in a team begins with sincere caring and sharing."

If honesty is important in your work relationships, include it in your **HIDDEN Agenda** for each meeting. Ask for honest feedback on the agenda items. When a comment from a co-worker indicates that a topic needs more time than you originally assigned to it, add the time or arrange to discuss it at another, specific time. This kind of concern and commitment will do more to increase productivity than any other single factor. Studies show that people respond favorably to fair, consistent treatment. This favorable response is a great way to start a meeting.

> **"Honesty is the best policy; but he who is governed by that maxim is not an honest man."**
> *Richard Whately, Archbishop of Dublin*

11

Integrity

Integrity is closely related to honesty. Standing up for your beliefs is a healthy way of asserting your vision and objectives. Asking each participant before or during a meeting what she or he thinks about the topic at hand assures your team that your meetings rely on open discussion. When integrity is respected, creativity abounds. Integrity fosters self-esteem. High self- and team esteem and high productivity are direct results of your **HIDDEN Agenda**.

Dignity

Dignity helps maintain the rapport you have developed through honesty and integrity. You want your meetings to be productive interactions. Your participants want to be free from sarcasm, humiliation, intimidation and discrimination. They want you to protect their egos and you want them to project their ideas. It's an even trade. A few examples follow:

- Humor works best when it is relevant to a meeting. If the purpose of your meeting is to brainstorm ways to improve customer service, then sketching a spiraling storm over each participant's corporate photograph is funny. But singling out one person's photograph with the sketch is discriminatory and may be perceived as a criticism of that person's thinking ability. Likewise, sarcasm and exaggeration may backfire. Saying, *"Pat would run over anyone who got between him and a new sales account"* may offend Pat or anyone else in the meeting. Most of us do not concentrate or contribute well once someone has been offended. Humor that attacks human dignity or that is racist, sexist or sacrilegious should be avoided.

- Discussing specific observations and behaviors in a meeting without naming an individual saves face.

> "A sense of humor ... is not so much the ability to appreciate humorous stories as it is the capacity to recognize the absurdity of the positions one gets into from time to time, together with skill in retreating from them with dignity."
>
> *Dana L. Farnsworth*

Avoid statements such as *"Shirley's newsletter is a waste of paper. Dumping it would give more paper to the other departments."* A better way to discuss redistributing the paper supply would be: *"If all departments conserve five reams of paper during the next month, we will have enough paper for the rest of the year."* With a general call for conservation, Shirley may be persuaded to limit the remaining issues of the newsletter!

- Individual performance reviews, warnings and firings are never appropriate in a public meeting. Were you ever reprimanded in public by a teacher or a parent? Remember the anger that burned in your eyes? When conducting your meetings, focus on positive behaviors for the public view. Save negative behaviors for private review. You will uphold dignity by maintaining privacy.

An estimated 20 million business meetings take place in America every day.

Development

Most people thrive in an atmosphere of honesty, integrity and dignity. This atmosphere is conducive to **development**, both personal and professional. Your meetings will be most effective when you make self- and team development part of your **HIDDEN Agenda**. Studies show that companies benefit the most from employees who set self-development goals and who list measurable, reasonable plans for achieving those goals. If the participants in your next meeting are faced with a dilemma, challenge them to set personal goals that will advance the company's goals. Encourage collaboration by recognizing strengths. For instance: *"Briana, you're studying warehouse management in your degree program, aren't you? Would you be willing to help our shipping and receiving department identify risk-management concerns? Your opinion would be appreciated."*

Look for ways in your meetings to link company goals to

a participant's development. Ask Gene to report on his experiences at the annual convention and to state how your company might use what he learned. Ask Sandra and Phil if they'd act as proofreaders for the secretarial pool when deadlines are tight. Encourage and expect people to volunteer for cross-training when their work orders relax. This cooperative spirit and personal recognition will build rapport within your team. Meetings will be pleasurable experiences when you create opportunities for participants to help one another grow.

Empowerment

Empowerment convinces members of your team that they can handle the challenges that arise. Once a problem is identified in the meeting, expect your team members to resolve it, and then do everything you can to meet their needs so they have the authority and resources to solve the problem. The biggest successes often come from taking the biggest risks. Encourage risk-taking by redefining failure in your meetings. Allow a failure to be a step toward success. Many failures miss being successes because someone gave up too soon. Let your meetings create future successes. If a report is incomplete in one meeting, ask the writer for a completion date and for an oral summary at another meeting, or ask for a written summary to be sent to all participants prior to the next meeting. Don't worry about people taking advantage of missing one meeting's deadline. They'll be grateful that you are willing to accommodate uncontrollable factors that interfere in their professional lives. Your attention and public recognition that the report is still expected to be completed are enough in most cases to get people on track. People typically perform well when given the space and the time to show what they can do.

A quality-assurance director in a large package-labeling plant explained how he empowers his staff and controls latecomers in his meetings. Lee uses a smile upon their arrival and these words: *"I'm glad you're here!"* Frequently, latecomers start to tell him their excuse for being gone. He says that an explanation is not necessary, that he trusts their judgment. He finishes with: *"Let's get to work."* Employees are empowered to make their own decisions and they live with the consequences of those decisions. Lee's staff has no need to abuse his trust, and he has no need to abuse theirs. They show up on time. This is a rare situation in most companies, but it need not be rare in your meetings. Trust participants to be there when the meeting starts. If they're not there at the beginning, begin without them and trust that they have a reason for being late or absent. If you take that attitude, people will willingly check in with you about what they missed and what they can do to prepare for the next meeting.

Needs Satisfaction

The sixth criterion for a successful meeting is **needs satisfaction**. Every meeting should have a purpose and a plan that meets participant needs. Otherwise, the meeting is a waste of time. Consider canceling a meeting if you have only general information on the agenda; send out a memo instead. You have seen how honesty, integrity, dignity, development and empowerment fit into the **HIDDEN Agenda**. Needs satisfaction summarizes these criteria: Meet your team's needs during the meetings, and members will meet your company's needs as best they know how. Actually, that's just about all any of us asks! With the six criteria in your **HIDDEN Agenda**, you'll have meetings that occur just often enough, that last just long enough and that accomplish more than enough. Your investment in meeting preparation will keep your audience awake and waiting for more.

Four-P Needs Assessment

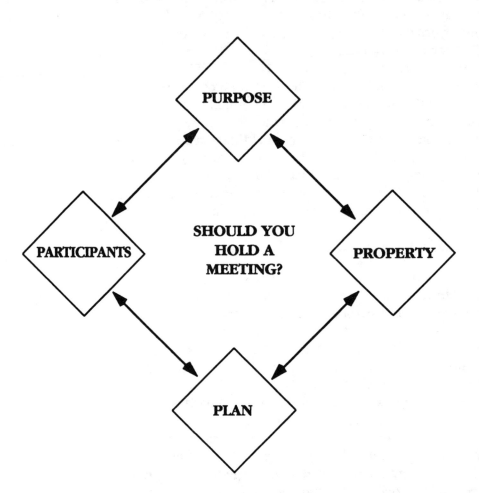

The **Four-P Needs Assessment** on the following page will guide you in deciding the fate and fortune of every meeting. Will the meeting evolve into a worthwhile use of space and time with a *purpose, participants, property* and a *plan?* If any of the four P's is missing, consider instead a memo, a facsimile, a phone call or a coffee break with the interested parties.

continued

Four-P Needs Assessment

ANSWER THE QUESTIONS IN THE FOUR CATEGORIES TO DETERMINE IF A MEETING IS NECESSARY.

PURPOSE:

What are the current conflicts, problems, concerns or time frames that a meeting could address?

What work and decisions must be completed before the meeting?

What information needs to be distributed?

What work or decisions must be completed during the meeting?

PARTICIPANTS:

Who are the people concerned with the meeting's agenda?

Who needs to do the work or make the decisions concerning the agenda?

Who needs this information?

Who needs to be present at the meeting?

PROPERTY:

What resources, facilities, materials, information or equipment are needed to accomplish the meeting's goal?

PLAN:

Could this work and decisions be accomplished through any of these alternative communications?
- memos, letters or reports
- facsimiles
- electronic mail
- voice mail or telephone calls
- teleconferences
- videotapes
- satellite conferences
- individual conversations

IF ANY OF THE P's IS MISSING, YOU'RE NOT READY TO CONDUCT A MEETING.
Consider postponing or eliminating the meeting until you have the reasons and the resources for people to meet with one another.

IF ALL OF THE P's ARE PRESENT, A MEETING IS NECESSARY!
Begin to plan your meeting with Chapter 2.

CHAPTER 2

Planning the Meeting

Congratulations! You have already saved time that is typically wasted. You have either avoided a meeting altogether or you have begun a well-organized plan for bringing people together.   Either way, people will be glad you are working toward quality meetings by minimizing the number and length of meetings when possible, eliminating a major frustration in the workplace.

Estimates suggest that managers spend between one-fourth and one-half of their workweek sitting in meetings or preparing for them, and that one-third of that time is wasted. Well-planned meetings could save at least 20 minutes in a one-hour meeting or six hours and 40 minutes in a week! Consider the participants' pay for the time you could save and you'll have a sense of how grateful your management will be. Eliminating meetings when possible also eliminates travel time and expenses, room and equipment costs, and preparation time, as well as

> *Industry Week* **reports that the estimated cost of wasted time in unproductive meetings exceeds $37 billion annually.**

unproductive transition time that accompanies every meeting. Wise documentation of these savings in dollars and hours will be a real advantage on your next performance appraisal! Knowing the primary purpose of a meeting will help you identify the kind of meeting to prepare. Here are four key purposes.

Four Purposes of Meetings

- To *inform* – to get or to give information

- To *form* – to make a decision or to solve a problem

- To *perform* – to complete a task

- To *conform* – to maintain a routine or a standard image

INFORM

The Inform Meeting

The focus of the **inform meeting** is its content. The participants learn the presented information, or you learn the requested information from the participants. Usually, the inform meeting uses discussion, queries, demonstrations, briefings and lecture to exchange information. Such a meeting usually can accommodate large groups of 10 or more participants.

FORM

The Form Meeting

The emphasis of the **form meeting** is the identification of concerns and the resolution of a conflict or a problem. Often, this kind of meeting uses discussion, brainstorming, persuasion and evaluation for developing a strategic plan. A group of three to nine participants works best in this meeting, because you need enough minds to create options, recognize probable consequences, test the criteria and select the best option. But, too many people can result in indecision and denial. Odd-numbered groups avoid tie votes. Both the size and the nature of this meeting lead to creative choices and realistic resolutions to a variety of concerns, conflicts and problems.

The Perform Meeting

The **perform meeting** centers on working as a team to get a task done. It may be a process, such as an evaluation, or a product, such as a flowchart. This kind of meeting lends itself to application, simulation and assignment. Small groups work best. This work session should focus on the desired results and the desired time frame. Several small groups may meet interdependently, with each group working on a selected aspect of the task. The key to success in work meetings is to minimize duplication or misunderstanding through clear communication among groups. Your position as meeting leader is to act as a communications liaison.

PERFORM

The Conform Meeting

The **conform meeting** is a routine meeting, based on tradition. It is a combination of the other three kinds of meetings. The focus is often status quo. Few people function at their highest level in a conform meeting. This kind of meeting seems to have more of a script than an agenda. Cancel one or two of these meetings to see if anyone misses or needs them. You may find that productivity increases as a direct result of this gift of time. If the participants are comfortable with this meeting, it may serve more of a social than a business function. Certainly, many fine community and professional organizations use the social atmosphere of this kind of meeting to set foundations for business goals. At its best, the conform meeting will develop a sense of identity and unity among participants that other kinds of meetings may not accomplish as well. Networking often evolves from this type of meeting. But don't fool yourself about its purpose!

CONFORM

All four types of meetings have their benefits and their limits. To help you determine which one suits your current needs, compare the **Four-P Assessment** with the **Meeting Summary Chart** that follows.

Meeting Summary Chart

Four Kinds	Primary Purpose	Focus	Size of Group
Inform Meeting	Giving and/or getting information	Content (learning)	Small or large group (2-100 participants)
Form Meeting	Making decisions or solving problems	Resolution (thinking)	Small or multiple groups (3-9 per group and 2-4 groups)
Perform Meeting	Completing a task	Results (doing)	Small or multiple groups (2-6 per group and 2-4 groups)
Conform Meeting	Maintaining a standard	Tradition/ image (being)	Small or large group (3-50 participants)

Now that you have determined the kind of meeting you need, you can turn your attention to the elements of the meeting.

Five Elements of a Meeting

Greeting: How you welcome the participants as they arrive

Opening: How you introduce the presenters, leaders, the objective, the agenda and the instructions

Delivery: How you present the content or concern, or how you organize the task

Closing: How you summarize decisions, make assignments, list recommendations, set deadlines and create action

Feedback: How you record the meeting, evaluate the process and check the progress of the items identified in the closing

Each of these elements is detailed in the following chapters. This brief overview gives you an idea of what to expect as you plan your meeting.

To continue preparing for your meeting, begin with the agenda. The **Four-P Needs Assessment** provides you with your starting point. What is it that you want to accomplish during the meeting? The answer to this question is your objective. The most productive meeting centers on one objective that avoids confusion and focuses your attention.

Three Guidelines for Stating Objectives of Meetings

- **Be specific and concrete.**

  What needs to be done by *when* and *how* and *where.*

- **Be positive and optimistic.**

  Expect success and avoid using negatives such as *not* and *never.*

- **Be realistic and practical.**

  Set an objective that is attainable and measurable.

Here are a few good examples of objectives:

- To improve safety at our main plant, each shift supervisor will recommend plans that can be implemented within one week for under $100 in total expenditures.

- To improve morale in the finance department, all participants will brainstorm 20 ways to build team spirit during the next 30 days.

- To conduct more effective meetings, each participant will evaluate his or her four most recent meetings based on criteria determined during the meeting.

With a clearly stated meeting objective, participants know the task at hand and assemble with a minimum of confusion and frustration. Some meetings have open-ended objective statements so the participants can help identify the specific criteria and/or the concrete results of the meeting. However, the more complete your objective statement is, the more focused your meeting will be.

Once you have your meeting objective, pose it as a question to the group. Participants will be more open to a question than to a command. Normally, we would all rather give answers than follow orders. When people are given choices, their personal investment in the outcome of a meeting rises. From that point, success is just a matter of time! Look at how the previous objective statements become welcome questions:

- What plans can we implement for under $100 to improve the safety at our main plant?

- What are 20 immediate ways of improving morale in our finance department?

- What are your criteria for determining effective meetings, what is your evaluation of the past four meetings, and what are your top two recommendations for changes?

Once your objective becomes a question, ask yourself if the answer is realistic for the time constraints. For instance, are five plans reasonable? If not, go for two or three. Are 20 ways reasonable? If not, go for 10 or 12. Are establishing criteria, testing them four times and selecting two recommendations reasonable? If not, go for three criteria, one test and one change.

The number of participants that you invite to the meeting will impact the amount of time it takes to complete the task. The more people invited, the more ideas suggested and the more time required. Now you are ready for the **Agenda Planning Worksheet**.

Agenda Planning Worksheet

What OBJECTIVE is served?

What BACKGROUND will explain the rationale for the objective?

What QUESTIONS need answers?	Estimate HOW LONG it will take to get these answers. (Include one-minute transitions and breaks as you shift from one agenda question to the next.)
1._____?	Number of minutes:_____
	Transition minute(s):_____
2._____?	Number of minutes:_____
	Transition minute(s):_____
3._____?	Number of minutes:_____
	Transition minute(s):_____

Total: _____agenda items   Total:____hours_____min.

You have enough information identified now to type a tentative agenda, such as the one below:

Tentative Agenda

Objective: To increase the effectiveness of our information meetings (2 min.)

Background: Lost time and effort are costly. The budget for this year is tight. Let's conserve expenses to protect our positions. Let's reduce frustration and confusion to project a winning team.

Agenda:

What are the most important criteria for determining effectiveness in our meetings? (10 min.)

What scale would best rate these criteria? (5 min.)

How have our last four meetings rated on this scale? (7 min.)

How can our meetings be changed to make them more effective? (8 min.)

What are the two best recommendations for changes in our next meeting? (8 min.)

Total agenda items: 5   Total time plus transitions: 45 minutes

Preparing a tentative agenda gives you a good idea of how much time you need to accomplish the stated objective and address agenda items. Given this information, which meeting mode will work best? The three most common modes are time sensitive.

Three Common Meeting Modes

- The **stand-up mode** allows participants to stand for the meeting, which is usually less than 15 minutes in length. Most people don't mind standing for a few minutes, and they sometimes welcome the change in perspective from sitting behind a desk. This is also called the "no" meeting: no coffee, no cookies, no chairs!

- The **sit-down mode** allows participants to sit for the meeting, which is usually 15 to 60 minutes in length. Most adults can sit for approximately an hour before needing a break to move around, although we all know exceptions to this rule. There are days when even 20 minutes of concentration is difficult for the best of us!

- The **move-around mode** permits participants to physically and periodically adjust their seating positions. Normally, strategic shifts in agenda items will provide natural opportunities for body shifts as well. Any meeting that lasts more than an hour must have accommodations for movement: a variety of tasks, training techniques, audio-visual aids and at least a 10-minute break for every 60 to 75 minutes the participants must sit. They need a reward for staying awake, so give them a break! If anyone falls asleep, then you all need a break from the snoring. Besides, by getting the kinks out of the bodies, you also get the kinks out of the minds.

How much floor space do you need for a stand-up meeting? How many chairs and tables (if the participants must write) do you need for a sit-down meeting? How much aisle space do you need for a move-around meeting? Check your local fire code for occupancy limits of conference rooms in your building or in any room you rent for your meetings. If your meetings are going to improve, then you must have room to work. Five adults seated behind an 8-foot table won't do! A good rule to follow is 3 feet by 2 feet of writing surface for every participant. Better to err with too much space than not enough space.

One more factor to consider in planning your meeting is figuring out the best time to meet. A few guidelines will help you know when to schedule your meeting.

> **Consultant Robert Lefton recalls a top-level managerial briefing in which discussion suddenly shifted to what kind of band to hire for a company function. They spent an hour and a half and $4,000 in managerial time on something they shouldn't have even been bothering with.**
> — *Training Development Journal*

Tips for Scheduling Meetings

- Ask key **participants** when they are available. Consider the *open house meeting* and the *staggered agenda meeting* to accommodate conflicting schedules. In an open house meeting, ask participants to stop by your office during a designated time frame to obtain or deliver written information. For a staggered agenda meeting, ask participants to be present only for the agenda item that requires their attention. Your agenda plan will help you know when to ask them to be at the meeting and for how long. Keeping to your agenda is crucial during the staggered agenda meeting.

- Check to find out when the **room** you need is available.

- Check your audio-visual resources if you need special **equipment** for your presentation, such as a videotape recorder/player and a television monitor.

- Check **travel** arrangements for participants.

- Avoid **peak productivity** time, such as Tuesday through Thursday mornings, unless you're scheduling a work session. Protect this time so that people can get their jobs done. Often, the hour before lunch or quitting time is productive because people avoid unnecessary delays that might otherwise extend the meeting time into their private lives.

- As a general rule, avoid Monday mornings, the mornings after holidays, Friday afternoons, the afternoons before holidays and the hour after lunch. People are in **transition** during these times. Their bodies may be present, but their brains may be off work.

- If you plan *periodic meetings* to discuss the **upcoming week**, consider Thursday afternoons. People are alert then. Waiting until Monday puts you behind before you start; holding it on Friday puts you in conflict with daydreams of the weekend.

- Consider **outside times** such as a breakfast meeting, a weekend retreat or a brief meeting while several of you carpool or walk together.

Use the guidesheets you already have (the **Four-P Needs Assessment,** the **Meeting Summary Chart,** the **Agenda Planning Worksheet** and your **Tentative Agenda**) and the one on the next page to plan your meeting. These guidesheets, coupled with decisions regarding time and space, will give you the basis for knowing your audience and promoting the meeting.

Meeting Plan

WHY will we meet? (Objective, background, kind of meeting.)

HOW MANY will attend? (Count the people you listed above.)
_____

WHO will attend? (Leader, presenters, participants, observers, others.)

WHAT will we do? (Objective, background, agenda items/ questions.)

WHEN will we meet? (Tentative date, day, time, duration.)

continued

Meeting Plan

WHERE will we meet? (Building/room, street address, telephone number, directions.)

HOW will we meet? (Mode, special arrangements such as brown bag lunch or exercise clothes.)

HOW MUCH will the meeting cost?

- Hourly rate of all participants and presenters: $ _____
- Rental fees for facilities and equipment: _____
- Travel expenses: _____
- Communication expenses: _____
- Materials expenses: _____
- Special accommodations such as refreshments: _____
- My preparation time: _____
- Other: _____

ESTIMATED COST: $ _____

C HAPTER 3

Knowing the Audience

Whether it's a group of executives or union employees, knowing your audience will equip you to promote the meeting, organize the presentation, manage the group and evaluate the entire meeting process. Your meeting is a live performance, just as if you were the director of a play. Your theatrical company is composed of actors, agents, producers and crew. Your responsibilities include not only the people on stage and behind the scene, but also the scene itself: set design, props, script revision, lighting, accommodations and equipment. You must have a vision of how a myriad of details intertwine in the final act. The plot progresses smoothly and characters develop fully when all the parts fit together. The biggest trick is to do this within the given time and cost constraints! And if your meeting isn't worth this much effort, it's probably not worth holding!

Directing the preparation, the presentation and the completion of an important meeting rivals the complexity of directing a movie. Trouble-shooting, decision-making, problem-solving and conflict resolution are some of the skills you need to run a meeting. The agenda acts as a script. Sometimes you provide your audience with some form of entertainment to add interest. Often, the characters you have to work with, literally and figuratively, fit into four behavioral categories, each with its representative prop. Within each behavioral category are five role players.

Four Behavioral Categories

Catalysts

The **catalysts** wave green flags. They include the personalities who encourage positive change, such as the *visionary*, the *seeker*, the *motivator*, the *teacher* and the *facilitator*.

Protectors

The **protectors** wave yellow flags. They include the personalities who urge us to be cautious and rational, such as the *caretaker*, the *caregiver*, the *cautionary*, the *advocate* and the *teaser*.

Adaptors

The **adaptors** wave white flags. They include the personalities who surrender to the situation, such as the *pleaser*, the *appeaser*, the *loyalist*, the *survivor* and the *opportunist*.

Resistors

The **resistors** wave red flags. They include the personalities who dislike change in the status quo,

"Blowing out the other fellow's candle won't make yours shine any brighter."

Anon.

including the *reactionary*, the *saboteur*, the *foot-dragger*, the *terrorist* and the *martyr*.

Although these categories and roles do not fit every circumstance, they do describe how people will respond differently given their own experiences and perspectives. Some people respond consistently and others do not. Yet, people often respond to new situations in these ways. Anticipating possible and probable responses to situations in your meetings will prepare you better.

If you know that Joe sometimes portrays the *martyr*, you may be able to counteract his resentment and resistance by lobbying for his support prior to the meeting, by asking his opinion on how to achieve the objective early in the meeting or by complimenting his integrity. Once you know that Jennifer sometimes chooses to play the *teaser*, you can call on her for an insightful laugh when tension or boredom runs high during an inform meeting. Ask the *facilitator* in Mel to help lead a small group while you lead another. Engage the *opportunist* in Donna to brainstorm ideas in your next form meeting.

Among the people you know will attend your meeting, who cast themselves into any of these roles or combinations of roles? Identify your **catalysts, protectors, adaptors** and **resistors** by listing their names beside their respective characteristic roles on the **"Role Call" Worksheet**.

"I don't say we all ought to misbehave, but we ought to look as if we could."

Orson Welles

"Role Call" Worksheet

Who, if anyone, in your organization fill the roles described below?

Catalysts

Role	Description	Person
Visionary:	one who leads with a clear vision for the future	_____
Seeker:	one who is a lifelong learner	_____
Motivator:	one who influences and encourages	_____
Teacher:	one who shares knowledge with others	_____
Facilitator:	one who removes obstacles	_____

Protectors

Role	Description	Person
Caretaker:	one who cares for property and things	_____
Caregiver:	one who cares how people are treated	_____
Cautionary:	one who is realistic and idealistic	_____
Advocate:	one who fights for the underdog	_____
Teaser:	one who plays the comic	_____

continued

"Role Call" Worksheet

Who, if anyone, in your organization fill the roles described below?

Adaptors

Role	Description	Person
Pleaser:	one who tries to accommodate everyone	_____
Appeaser:	one who makes peace no matter what	_____
Loyalist:	one who denies any change	_____
Survivor:	one who actively chooses self over others	_____
Opportunist:	one who actively seizes the situation	_____

Resistors

Role	Description	Person
Reactionary:	one who impulsively reacts	_____
Saboteur:	one who is a covertly aggressive complainer	_____
Foot-dragger:	one who reluctantly follows	_____
Terrorist:	one who is an openly aggressive antagonizer	_____
Martyr:	one who is a silent, misunderstood idealist	_____

Identify the power of the role and borrow its strength to reach your meeting's objective. Your **HIDDEN Agenda** comes into focus when you get to know your audience. Sometimes people play more than one role at a time, and sometimes they appear not to be playing any role. Whatever the case, all people bring at least eight personal dimensions to your meeting.

Modern psychologists, sociologists, neurologists and educators have constructed many models for analyzing behavior and thinking styles. A composite of several models suggests eight personal dimensions that interact and react in unique combinations to create each individual.

Eight Personal Dimensions

- **Mental Dimension:**
  emotions and intellect

- **Physical Dimension:**
  sensations and movement

- **Social Dimension:**
  introspection and interaction

- **Political Dimension:**
  realism, pragmatism and idealism·

- **Sensory Dimension :**
  auditory and visual preferences

- **Creative Dimension:**
  originality and interpretation

- **Active Dimension :**
  experiences, details, results and options

- **Motivational Dimension :**
  self-direction and other-direction

To decide which of these dimensions dominates in you, take the following quick quiz.

Personal Dimension Awareness Indicator

On each line below, circle the statement in either the left or the right column that best describes you (or the person you are profiling) most of the time. The center column notes the dimension(s) for your reference.

DIMENSION(S)

I am emotional.	(mental)	*I am intellectual.*
I am spontaneous.	(mental)	*I am restrained.*
I prefer ideas and concepts.	(mental)	*I prefer things and images.*
I prefer global thinking.	(creative/mental)	*I prefer sequential thinking.*
I am more aware of sensation.	(physical)	*I am more aware of movement.*
I use intuition more.	(mental/physical)	*I use evidence more.*
I prefer sight.	(sensory)	*I prefer sound.*
I prefer sight.	(sensory/physical)	*I prefer touch.*
I prefer sound.	(sensory/physical)	*I prefer touch.*
I prefer working alone.	(social/motivational)	*I prefer working with a partner.*
I prefer small groups.	(social)	*I prefer large groups.*
I am a realist.	(political)	*I am an idealist.*
I prefer the practical choice.	(political)	*I prefer the easiest, fastest choice.*
I prefer excellence.	(political/active)	*I prefer action.*
I prefer to listen.	(sensory/mental)	*I prefer to watch.*
I prefer music with words.	(mental)	*I prefer music without words.*
I prefer reading.	(creative/mental)	*I prefer art or math.*
I prefer oral demonstrations.	(sensory)	*I prefer written instructions.*
I prefer making something new.	(mental/creative)	*I prefer taking something apart.*
I prefer details.	(active/creative)	*I prefer options.*
I prefer experiences.	(physical/active)	*I prefer results.*
I prefer details.	(mental/active)	*I prefer results.*
I prefer experiences.	(active/creative)	*I prefer options.*
I am self-motivated.	(motivational)	*I am motivated by others.*
I am more pensive.	(mental/physical)	*I am more physical.*
I am more social.	(social/political)	*I am more political.*
I prefer doing one task.	(creative/mental)	*I prefer multiple tasks.*

(Note: *This is not a tested psychological device.*)

Use this survey as a discussion starter for participants in a meeting. You may want to include other pairs of behaviors that are pertinent to your team, such as *I prefer to speak on the phone* and *I prefer to speak with people in person.* You may even want to use a few pairs as a mini-survey as part of your promotion or opening for a meeting. Ask participants to answer the survey and use one response as a way of introducing themselves to the group. You'll quickly realize how complex each person is and how difficult it is to categorize individuals. We are a mix of all eight dimensions. The following **Audience Analysis Worksheet** will also help you get to know those attending your meeting.

Audience Analysis Worksheet

Rate the expected members in the categories listed below.

		High			Low	
		4	3	2	1	Unknown
1.	Knowledge of the topic	—	—	—	—	—
2.	Technical vocabulary	—	—	—	—	—
3.	Openness to new ideas	—	—	—	—	—
4.	Commitment to this meeting	—	—	—	—	—
5.	Oral communication skills	—	—	—	—	—
6.	Diversity of education	—	—	—	—	—
7.	Diversity of culture and values	—	—	—	—	—
8.	Diversity of experience	—	—	—	—	—
9.	Team effort	—	—	—	—	—
10.	Attention span	—	—	—	—	—
11.	Flexibility	—	—	—	—	—
12.	Self-confidence	—	—	—	—	—
13.	Attention to detail	—	—	—	—	—
14.	Sociability	—	—	—	—	—
15.	Energy level	—	—	—	—	—
16.	Competency and skill	—	—	—	—	—
17.	Consistency	—	—	—	—	—
18.	Assertiveness	—	—	—	—	—

Audience Profile Score Total = _____
(High = 60+, Average = 45-50)

Now that you really know your audience, it's important for participants to be enthusiastic about the meeting. To motivate your audience, show them how they will benefit individually and collectively from this meeting. Complete the **Needs Satisfaction Worksheet** in preparation for giving your audience a better, briefer meeting.

"The only meeting that ever started on time was held up an hour while things were explained to people who came in late and didn't know what was going on."

Doug Larson

Needs Satisfaction Worksheet

What does the audience need to know?

What does the audience want to know?

What are the possible benefits of a successful meeting for the audience?

What questions will the audience have?

C HAPTER 4

Promoting the Meeting

"No matter how great a warrior he is, a chief
cannot do battle without his Indians."

Anon.

You can increase the effectiveness of any meeting by
inviting the participants to get involved. They will be more
open to your leadership because you bothered to ask for
their opinions, suggestions and assistance. An opportune
time for making these individual contacts with your
audience is when you have completed preliminary plans
and you are ready to promote the meeting. Promoting the
meeting involves creating excitement both before and

during the event itself. Use these two important factors in your promotion:

- **display care and concern** for the audience and ...
- give participants **opportunity to control and choose** what happens.

The first of these factors was discovered in 1927 in Hawthorne, Illinois. Researchers made environmental changes in the working conditions of five women who assembled telephone relays for the Western Electric Company. When the researchers adjusted the lighting, the women's productivity rose. When the researchers shortened the length of the workweek, the women's output remained high. As the researchers added one variable, they subtracted another. Always the women's productivity remained higher than the rate of a similar group working under normal factory conditions. After two years of changes the researchers suggested that the women's consistently high productivity showed that they felt special. Someone cared enough to change their world in an effort to improve it. The researchers' conclusions became known as the Hawthorne effect.

Years later, another researcher rediscovered and broadened the significance of that experiment. From additional data in the original study, he determined the second factor – having the opportunity to control what happens. The five women apparently had counters to mark the progress of their efforts for the researchers! They were paid by the piece rather than by the hour. To earn more, each worked faster. Each had some choice and some control over her work. Current information, excellent instruction and target incentives combined with a caring atmosphere will increase productivity. The same is true for meetings.

We all work better when we feel better and when we have input in the meeting agenda. Consistent, immediate feedback during a meeting is an essential communication skill. And positive, intermittent reinforcement is the most important form of feedback. When that occasional comment of support, encouragement or praise arrives, it makes your meetings successful.

Although every meeting should offer care, concern and choices, not every meeting needs to be a "main event." A few hints will help you promote an important meeting.

The Big, Bright, Bold, Bang Approach to Events

BIG: **Exaggerate everything from gestures to guests. Think BIG.**

BRIGHT: **Use lots of color to evoke happy feelings and curiosity.**

BOLD: **Keep information short and easy to read with large print and borders on posters. Use pictures to draw attention.**

BANG: **Project plenty of noise and loud voices to draw attention to your approaching event.**

Create a **Big, Bright, Bold, Bang** event at least once a year. For the other meetings, use the following ideas to promote interest and investment in them.

Tips for Promoting Meetings

- Include inspirational quotations, cartoons or jokes on your memos.

- Wear a costume that represents the meeting's objective.

- Perform a skit to highlight the objective.

- Ask everyone to wear a certain color to the meeting to promote team-building. (One business professional especially likes "Purple Underwear Day." She places purple boxer shorts over her shirt sleeve inside her jacket – just in case someone wants to check!)

- Organize a potluck lunch before an afternoon meeting.

- Ask participants to make brief reports on their recent travels or achievements.

- Hand out party invitations or advance tickets to announce the meeting.

- Send a piece of a puzzle or a whole puzzle minus one piece to each participant. The picture or message on the puzzle should be pertinent to the meeting so that it can be assembled during the greeting or the opening.

- Make a video or audiotape of your promotional pitch or provide a special viewing of a video immediately following the meeting.

- Create decorations and displays to attract interest. Usually a centerpiece or one focal point is all you need.

- Hire an event planner or a consultant to help you think of more ideas.

Use the guidesheets that follow to plan your meeting communications schedule and strategy. The **Communications Timeline** and the **Survey Agenda** will help you keep your audience informed and involved in the meeting even before it starts. These guidesheets will help you to *display care and concern* while giving your audience an *opportunity to control and choose* what happens in part of their meeting.

Communications Timeline

Target Date: **Task:**

_____ **Preliminary Planning:** Complete the **Four-P Needs Assessment, Agenda Planning Guide, Tentative Agenda** and **Meeting Plan.** You will usually spend one hour of preparation for every hour of meeting time.

_____ **Initial Contact:** Check with people before deciding on a meeting time. If you are asking someone to prepare something, either oral or written, give at least a week's notice for each hour of presentation.

_____ **Reservations:** Reserve equipment and facilities as needed. Check room capacity (especially if the group is large) and accessibility (especially if new or physically impaired members will attend).

_____ **Announcement:** Send a written notice about the meeting and a request for confirmation of attendance along with a copy of the previous minutes, background information for the meeting and the current **Tentative Agenda** or **Survey Agenda.** Do this one week in advance for each hour of meeting time scheduled.

_____ **Promotion:** Decide if this meeting needs additional buildup and, if so, when and how.

_____ **Confirmations:** Call participants for delinquent confirmations and confirm your reservations for facilities and equipment.

_____ **Reminder Contact:** Make a reminder memo or call one day ahead for each hour of meeting scheduled.

_____ **Materials:** Prepare all materials, such as transparencies and handouts, the week before a big meeting or two days before a short one. Remember to include the final agenda.

_____ **Equipment and Room Check:** Make a check one day before a big meeting or an hour before a short meeting. Test the equipment and check the seating arrangement.

_____ **MEETING**

_____ **Thank-You Notes/Calls:** Write notes or call helpful participants to express your appreciation the day after the meeting.

_____ **Minutes:** Within two days after the meeting, reproduce the record.

_____ **Progress Checks:** Within one day to one week after the meeting, check with the parties responsible for completing the action plan.

Survey Agenda

(Send this to participants three to seven days prior to the meeting.)

Please recommend changes and additions by (date)_____
(Suggest two days before the meeting.)

Send this information to:
    (List your name.)_____
    (List your mailing address or mail stop.)_____
    (List your phone and/or fax numbers.)_____

WHY we need to meet: (Write your objective here.)

WHO should meet: (List those people who need to be at the meeting.)

WHEN we will meet:
    (State the day and date.)_____
    (State the times.) _____ a.m./p.m. to _____ a.m./p.m.

WHERE we will meet:
    (State the address and directions as needed.)
        Room:_____
        Building:_____
        Street Address:_____
        Directions (or attach map):_____

WHAT questions we will answer: (List agenda questions.)

What else do you WANT to know?

What else do you WONDER about?

THANK YOU!

*C*HAPTER 5

Organizing the Presentation

"As a vessel is known by its sound, whether it be cracked or not; so men are proved by their speeches, whether they be wise or foolish."

Demosthenes

If you had to choose among running the Boston Marathon, volunteering to chair the next fund-raising drive, scrubbing the office coffee pot and preparing the coffee each morning for a month, cleaning three stories of windows, babysitting 28 of your co-workers' children at the annual picnic, completing 154 cold calls or making a presentation, which would be your least favorite? Chances are it would be to make a presentation. To organize and deliver presentations may cause anxiety or outright fright. Some people say they'd rather face death than get up in front of a group and talk!

Yet, getting up in front of a group and talking is part of conducting a meeting. Sometimes you can delegate the actual presentation to someone else. Or, maybe you'll be so lucky that someone volunteers. Perhaps you've made it this far in the business world without tripping over your tongue or stumbling through your notes. If not, welcome to the club. The tips in this chapter will help you and your audience have a positive presentation.

The secret is to take one step at a time. **Nine Essential E's of Speaking** and **Eight Ways to Develop a Topic** will take you through the process. The image and rehearsal tips will help you polish your style. What will you gain? Increased confidence and competence! Let's begin by identifying the characteristics of effective speaking.

Nine Essential E's of Speaking

1. Build Esteem

2. Arrive Early

3. Be Enthusiastic

4. Make Eye Contact

5. Provide Experiences

6. Give Evidence

7. Show Empathy

8. End on Time

9. Evaluate Strengths

> "A flow of words is no proof of wisdom."
>
> *Anon.*

Build Esteem

Good preparation and organization will increase your self-confidence. It's easier to expect success when you're ready for it. With each successful meeting, you build a reputation. Your co-workers will trust you to put together an effective and efficient meeting each time you conduct one. One important aspect is to prepare to greet the members by name, if possible. Arrange to meet any members you don't already know before the meeting begins. Nothing builds esteem quite so quickly as someone who makes the effort to know everyone's name.

Arrive Early

Get to the meeting place 15 minutes to an hour before the meeting begins. If you're familiar with the room and you're planning a simple meeting, a few minutes is all you'll need to assess and adjust the equipment, the visual displays, the seating, the temperature and the ventilation. If you're unfamiliar with the room or you're planning a complex meeting, allow more time for controlling the environment. Too many meetings have failed because the room was too warm or too cool for comfort, there weren't enough chairs, the speaker had to search for materials or members couldn't see the displays or hear the speaker well. Most of these complaints are easy to handle if you arrive early. Also, you'll want to get to the meeting place first to have time to assess and adjust yourself. Check your appearance in a mirror, get a glass of water if you'll be talking a lot and take a few deep breaths to relax. Be ready to begin the meeting on time, using a wall clock or the group's synchronized watches, and begin on time!

> "I have always been a quarter of an hour before my time, and it has made a man out of me."
>
> *Horatio Nelson*
>
> "Also, a superb admiral."
>
> *ibid.*

Be Enthusiastic

Your energy and interest levels directly influence your audience's attention level. Know what you will say, how you will say it and when you will say it. Your attention to the purpose of the meeting will ensure your audience's attention. If you are nervous about speaking and think it will interfere with your effectiveness, here's a secret tactic to use.

Give yourself permission to admit your fear to your audience and then commit to do your best. You might say: *"I'm nervous about being in front of you today. Public speaking is a new skill I'm learning. Perhaps jumping over the Grand Canyon on a motorcycle or splitting an arrow stuck in a target would be easier. But, I'm told that our company doesn't need any more motorcyclists or archers! Yet, we do need risk takers. So, I'm here today to do my best for you."* People respond well to such honesty. And they're glad you're in front of the group, rather than themselves.

Moving around occasionally will help you to relax and the participants to listen. Although you want to conduct a successful meeting and not necessarily an entertaining one, a few laughs or smiles help your audience listen better and you present better. Some speakers pace their meeting, making sure they break long monologues and discussions every seven to 10 minutes throughout a presentation to keep their audiences tuned in. A relaxed atmosphere encourages learning, sharing, questioning and creating. Decision-making and problem-solving thrive on enthusiasm. Being optimistic and positive opens possibilities, options and resolutions that might be overlooked otherwise. The bottom line is this: If you're bored presenting, you can bet your audience is bored listening!

Make Eye Contact

In some cultures, such as those of Orientals and Native Americans, it is impolite and disrespectful to look a person in the eye. However, in today's American business culture, making eye contact is a sign of good manners and respect. Audiences expect this treatment, and they resent and distrust speakers who avoid it. If you are uncomfortable speaking in front of a group, the following tips will help.

Tips for Making Eye Contact

- In your mind, divide your audience into *quadrants*. Select a seat or a friendly person in the left front section, one in the right front section, one in the left back and another in the right back. These are your focal points. Rotate among them to give your audience the feeling that you are speaking to everyone. If you arrive early, you can select these spots before anyone fills a chair.

- While talking with friends, practice looking at their *foreheads*. It appears as if you're making eye contact, yet you'll be less nervous than if you really were looking directly into their eyes.

- Draw an *imaginary line* just above the heads of the audience. Speak to this line, moving your eyes slowly around it and back.

- Use *visual displays* so that you can see key points along with your audience. This will keep your eyes focused upward rather than buried in your notes.

- If you do use *notes*, write reminders to look up briefly and regularly and to pause periodically to emphasize a point, to make a shift or to study your audience's response. These notes also will remind you to keep your head up so that your voice will project better.

Offer Experiences

Offering experiences is the fifth "E" of speaking. Get people involved in your agenda or program within the first few minutes of the meeting. Three ways to do this are by telling stories, using analogies and planning activities. The trick to making your meeting memorable is to elicit the emotions and senses of your audience. Allow members to participate through personal descriptions of events, including feelings, sights, sounds and movement. Ask Janice to describe her misadventures in Chicago as she gathered the data for today's meeting. Allow members to anticipate both intellectual and emotional shifts in your presentation by making choices about activities or methods. Ask Warren if he'd prefer to act as recorder or leader for the group. Ask the participants if they'd rather work on a task with the entire group or in small groups. Explain how a fresh concept is similar to a familiar concept by using analogies, such as "conducting a meeting is like directing a scene on a stage." Remember to keep all stories, analogies and activities focused on the current objective. Stories are powerful and effective tools in making your meeting positive, but remember that it's crucial that the meeting end by the agreed time. Don't let a long story sidetrack your agenda.

Give Evidence

Provide proof, background, definitions and rationale for your agenda. Use verified facts and observations to support your statements of purpose or concern. Interpret statistics fairly by stating their value as well as their limits. For example, *"During the second quarter, we raised our revenues 18 percent over this year's first quarter figure and lowered them 2 percent compared to last year's second quarter figure."* Make evidence as specific and concrete as possible so people can easily understand it. Another example is, *"This means that we've had some success in our new marketing plan and that we must continue to find ways to increase our visibility. Let's look for publicity opportunities. Would each of you identify something or someone in your work area that we could publicize in the news media?"*

Show Empathy

Be considerate of your participants. Keep in mind their professional and personal needs. Give participants the information and the direction that they need to do their jobs as well as they can. Give them a break if attention lags or if bladders call! Your preparation in assessing needs, planning the meeting and knowing the audience gives you a basis for understanding the members' attitudes, feelings and experiences. Note: The mind can obtain only what the seat can endure!

> **Words are but wind, but seeing is believing.**
>
> *Proverb*

End on Time

Two excuses for failing to end a meeting on time are legitimate. The first is that the group agrees to continue the meeting beyond its scheduled end in order to avoid rescheduling or to preserve the group's momentum. And the second reason is that you finish early! Announce the meeting's ending time on all communications sent to those expected to attend and repeat it at the opening of the meeting. When people are held captive in meetings, they become resentful and uncooperative, which interferes with constructive communication. It's as if the meeting leader is saying, *"My responsibilities are more important than yours."* This may or may not be true, but members do not want to feel that you disregard their schedules. If members often leave meetings early, ask for their commitment to stay through the designated time. This will be your contract with them to stay through the entire meeting – as long as you end the meeting early or on time. Avoid a dispute by agreeing at the beginning of the meeting to use a certain clock, watch or timer to keep track of the time.

Evaluate Strengths

If you are new at conducting meetings, be gentle with yourself about what you did well and what you want to work on. Effective change takes time. Be positive in your comments and language when describing what you want to improve. Tell yourself what you want to do next time, rather than what you do not want to do again.

Typical response:

"I messed up. Why can't I get this right? I was so scared that I forgot to look at them enough. I misplaced the second handout and the bulb in the projector burned out. I felt my voice tremble and my face flush. I must have looked like a fool!"

Positive response:

"I made some improvements. I arrived early and ended three minutes early. We accomplished the objective and have a workable action plan in place. I spoke loudly enough, and the group even laughed a couple of times. Next time, I want to remember to organize the handouts in the order I'll give them to the group. Also, I want to think of a few quips I can respond with when the unexpected happens. To calm myself, I'll take a sip of water and a couple of deep breaths before the meeting and a few times during natural pauses."

If you want members to evaluate your efforts and the meeting's content, present the evaluation questions or items in positive language to encourage constructive responses. We know all too well what our weaknesses are. We often try so hard to avoid them or to hide them that we limit the energy we have to make the positive changes. Instead of asking *"What did I do wrong?"*, ask *"What would you like done differently next time?"* Allow yourself to feel good about the parts of the meeting that you did well. Reassure yourself that you'll continue to make the necessary change the best you can. This sense of success will help you build more successful meetings in the future. The **Nine Essential E's of Speaking** will improve your presentation as will the following **Eight Ways to Develop a Topic**.

Knowing what you'll say, how you'll say it and when you'll say it is crucial in your preparation. Developing a topic means writing notes or a script for your presentation. You will want to answer as many of your audience's questions as possible while you're giving the presentation. This saves time because it clarifies many uncertainties before they spawn confusion. A well-developed topic also provides a realistic picture of the objective at hand and increases the chances for creative decisions.

Eight Ways to Develop a Topic

- DIRECT
- AIDA
- Seven W's
- Listing
- Looping
- Outlining
- Mapping
- Flowcharting

DIRECT

The **DIRECT** approach is a six-part system that forms an acrostic, a word in which each letter represents an idea. This approach refers to *definitions, illustrations, relationships, experiences, circumstances* and *testimonials.* It encourages you to think about your topic in ways you may have overlooked.

What **d**efinitions will the audience need to know to understand this topic?

What **i**llustrations, both visual and verbal, would help?

What **r**elationships such as comparisons, causes, effects or steps exist?

What **e**xperiences such as stories, activities or grouping would help?

What **c**ircumstances such as facts, observations or conditions exist?

What **t**estimonials or quotations would influence the audience?

AIDA

AIDA is an acronym, a word created from the first letters of a series of words. It represents *attention, interest, desire* and *action.* Advertisers and marketers use this model to design sales and promotional materials. Because you are "selling or promoting" a meeting, this model will work for you.

> **THE SHOCK TECHNIQUE**
>
> "My secret in gaining attention was to turn the obvious into the scandalous by stating it plainly."
>
> *H.L. Mencken*

What will get your audience's **attention?**

What will hold their **interest?**

What will arouse their **desire** to commit to the meeting plan?

What **action** do you want and how will you get it?

The better you know your audience and your subject, the easier this is to do. If you do a good job promoting your meeting, you will have gone a long way toward getting the audience's attention and commitment already. Keeping your meeting on schedule will also focus their attention. Making sure your meeting has a distinct, defined purpose will hold their interest. Getting them all involved in discussions and decisions will build desire. Asking them for their expertise and opinions will encourage them to act. Your agenda corresponds to this model. Now use the same process for your topic.

Seven W's

The **Seven W's** include the five traditional questions – *who, what, when, where* and *why* – and two more – *want* and *wonder*. You saw this approach when you worked on the agenda.

Who needs to know about this topic or who is involved in it?

What is this topic, based on definition, experience or analysis?

When is this topic relevant or how is it placed in history?

Where is this topic found or where is it important?

Why is this topic important?

What else do you *want* your audience to know?

What else will your audience still *wonder* about?

Use the seven W-words shown here as headings for your

topic development. Put them on a flip chart, a marker board or a transparency for use during your presentation. You may want to combine this system with the DIRECT approach or the AIDA model. All three systems work well together.

Listing

Listing involves brainstorming ideas and points of interest about the topic, deciding which ones you'll use and then arranging them in a logical order. The advantage of this method is that it's simple and fast. The disadvantage is that you may forget to include something important or interesting. Listing may be combined with any of the three previous ways to develop a topic. A list of key words may be all you need to serve as notes during an oral presentation. These notes could become a handout or a visual aid. If you want more than a few key words as notes, write or type a script with wide margins and triple-spaced lines. The extra space makes your script easier to read.

> **THE BRAIN**
> "Not only the greatest computer ever devised, but the only one produced by unskilled labor."
>
> *Bob Considine*

Looping

Looping takes a list of key words that are arranged in a logical order and develops each word into a written or spoken paragraph. The first key word is linked to the second key word in the first paragraph, the second to the third in the second paragraph and so on until the final word loops back to the first word. This illustration shows how it works.

> Looping *is my favorite way to begin writing a presentation because the system has a clear beginning and end, and it's fun. I enjoy watching the circular pattern evolve as I link key thoughts into a logical* development.
>
> *The* development *of any presentation is important if the leader wants the audience to understand and to participate in decisions involving the presented material. One way to help participants follow your ideas is to provide them with clear and frequent* transitions.

65

Transitions *are markers, words or phrases that tell your audience how you get from one main idea to the next or how you explain a main idea. Examples of these markers are "for example," "however," "therefore" and "finally, the third point I want to make is...." Well-placed and well-defined transitions help your presentation style* flow.

In addition, this flow *is achieved by the repetition of one key word from the end of a paragraph to the beginning of the next paragraph. This repetition guides the participants' thinking as you present your material. It also provides a built-in system for unifying your introduction with your conclusion by eventually bringing your audience back to the first key word. No other topic development does this as well as* looping.

Outlining

Outlining is a traditional development tool that most of us learned early in school. The worst part of outlining is thinking of two subheadings for every heading. The next awful task is getting the corresponding details lined up! Here's a hint.

Instead of this: *Do this:*

I. _____ + _____

  A. _____   • _____

   1. _____   – _____

   2. _____   • _____

  B. _____   • _____

II. _____   – _____

           – _____

Using the graphic symbols instead of the traditional numbers and letters will free you to think about the content, rather than its sequence and format. It doesn't matter whether your columns match or your Arabic numbers follow your Roman numerals. Develop your ideas by using the graphic symbols of your choice to represent each level of detail.

Mapping

Mapping shows levels of detail similar to outlining. To use mapping as a development tool, use key words and connectors within the topic diagram. An example of mapping looks similar to a family tree.

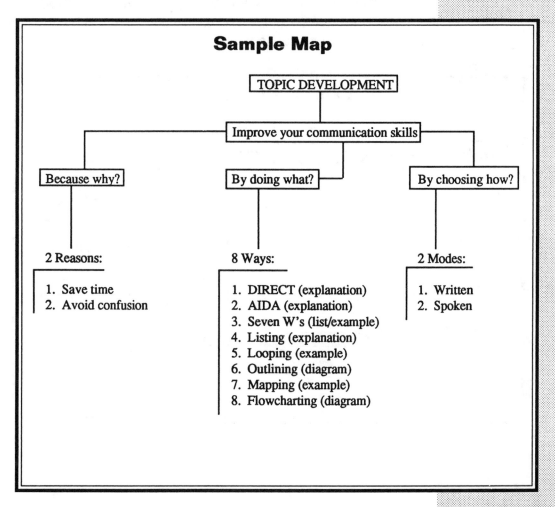

Sample Map

TOPIC DEVELOPMENT

Improve your communication skills

Because why?   By doing what?   By choosing how?

2 Reasons:

1. Save time
2. Avoid confusion

8 Ways:

1. DIRECT (explanation)
2. AIDA (explanation)
3. Seven W's (list/example)
4. Listing (explanation)
5. Looping (example)
6. Outlining (diagram)
7. Mapping (example)
8. Flowcharting (diagram)

2 Modes:

1. Written
2. Spoken

Flowcharting

The eighth way to develop a topic is **flowcharting**. For each function of the information given use a different shape in a diagram. Use a rectangle, for instance, to represent a main point, use an oval for a definition, a circle for an example, a triangle for a cause or any shapes you choose for specific information functions. Use connecting lines to show the flow from one function to the next.

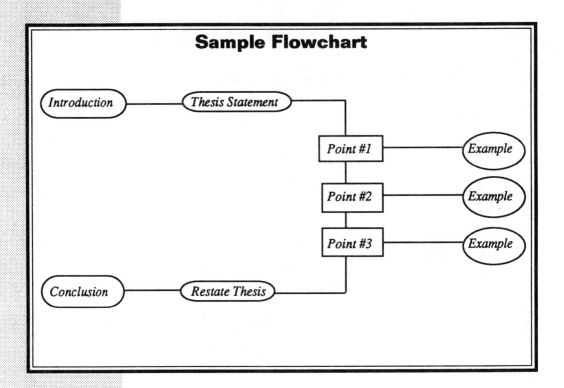

Sample Flowchart

This flowchart indicates that the introduction and the conclusion in this presentation are similar, three main points are stated, and three examples. The lines show the sequence, moving from the introduction through all the points and supporting details to the conclusion.

Whether you prefer notes or diagrams, you must find several ways to develop your topic. If you hit a writer's block, simply use one of these methods to get unblocked. You will discover that some topics lend themselves better to one way than another. For example, a progress report or a proposal may be presented best as a chronological flowchart that moves through background information to the current situation and into recommendations for the future. The DIRECT approach offers a variety of information, and the AIDA model focuses on the audience's perception. Each method will help provide a clear, concise and convincing presentation.

*C*HAPTER 6

Rehearsing the Presentation

Having a well-prepared presentation will increase your confidence. Part of preparation is composing and organizing the material you must cover in the meeting. Another part of preparation is composing and organizing yourself! This chapter offers tips for presenting your visual and vocal image. Then you'll see how these images interact as you use the rehearsal tips.

How you present yourself is as important as how you present your topic. Your visual image projects a message even before your voice does. One favorite social-behavior study tested the public's bias toward well-groomed, attractive people. In the study, several men and women appear well groomed and attractive in some photographs and frumpy, severe and unattractive in others. The public perceived the attractive people as more competent and confident than the unattractive people, not realizing the photographs were of the same people. Some people said they'd give the well-groomed people higher salaries and more chances to overcome failures. In almost all instances, well-groomed, attractive people have the advantage. So, take the time to look good!

Visual Image Tips

- As you prepare to talk, people will focus on your **face**. Check your hair, your makeup, your collar and your shoulders for any distractions such as labels, smudges and lint.

- Avoid jewelry, ties or other **accessories** that draw attention. You'll want the audience's attention on what you're saying, rather than on what you're wearing.

- Wear solid **colors**, subtle plaids or small-scaled prints in predominantly neutral and cool shades, such as grays and blues. These calm colors will help you look and feel in control. Large prints can distract and appear to add weight. Wear comfortable, stylish clothing that allows you to move, yet fits smoothly.

- Nothing hurts worse than **shoes** that are uncomfortable. Choose your shoes for the meeting based on comfort as well as appearance. Cushion your insoles to give a spring to your step.

- If you are short, stand on a riser. Stand behind a lectern only if you're on a step stool. If your audience can see only your shifting eyes and the top of your head, it won't matter what you plan to say – you won't be heard over the snickers. If you are tall, you may want to sit on a stool so that your face is at a comfortable **height** for the seated audience members to see. Strained necks will shorten their attention span.

- Your **posture** is a direct gauge of your command over an audience. When you stand and sit straight, your audience assumes you think and talk straight, too.

- **Smile** occasionally and appropriately. Smiling all the time will confuse people. Generally, it's best to smile after the introductions when you're meeting someone for the first time. People take you more seriously after knowing your name.

- **Consult** with a professional image counselor for more ideas that are specific to you.

Your vocal image is as important as your visual image. If your vocal characteristics are unpleasant – monotone, shrill or nasal – people will hear only the sound of your voice, not your words. If your speech is too loud, too soft, too fast or too slow, people will quit listening. If your audience has to work at understanding your words, they'll give up and let you talk to yourself. Some tips follow.

Vocal Image Tips

- **Tape** yourself having a conversation with a friend. Listen for speech mannerisms such as fillers, inflections and rate. *"Um"* and *"OK"* repeated 26 times in 60 seconds is irritating. You may not hear these repetitions until you listen to a tape! One man years ago said, *"Don't you know what I mean?"* after every other sentence. He became offended when others brought it to his attention. Only a recording is believable. Use this recording to time and mark 30 seconds. Count the words you speak during that time. As a general rule, a comfortable listening rate is two to three words per second. If you speak only one word per second, practice talking faster because people will fall asleep. If you speak more than three words per second, practice talking slower because no one understands you.

- Drink **water** before and during vocal exercise. Keep your throat lubricated. Avoid carbonated or alcoholic beverages because they cause burping and slurring.

- Lower your pitch to appear calm and in **command**. While listening to the radio on the way to work this week, practice singing along in a lower octave. Another way to be in command is to use short, assertive statements such as *"I need your help now"* or *"We need a decision now."*

- Breathe from your abdomen in slow, deep breaths. This relaxes your upper body to allow a rich sound that projects easily. Also, open the back of your throat when you talk. You can feel this when you open your mouth and tilt your chin upward. Again, this helps you **project** your voice.

- Practice the sounds of your **enthusiasm**. A vivid, vivacious voice is impossible to ignore.

- Practice **pronouncing** the total word. Lazy speech suggests a lazy mind or at least a tired mouth. Don't say *gonna* for *going*, *sketti* for *spaghetti* and *coulda* for *could have.*

- **Consult** a speech therapist or an experienced speaker for more ideas.

You've now prepared notes or a script for your presentation and you've made conscious choices to project a confident image. Practicing your actual presentation comes next. This is the polish that makes your hard work shine and your meeting flow.

Rehearsal Tips

- Write out **key words** or a script for your presentation.
- Read or recite it **silently** before going further.
- Drink approximately one-half glass of **water** to lubricate your throat and voice before speaking. Drink the other half of your water as you read or recite your presentation aloud. If your speech is short, you may not need the extra water. It's smart to have it ready just in case your throat feels as if someone is choking you or you are choking on your words! Also, by needing water your body will tell you when you've been talking too long without a break!
- **Summarize** your main points aloud as if responding to a question.
- **Define** key terms aloud as if your audience has asked for them.
- **Tape** your speaking part. Time it. Shorten or expand it.
- **Listen** to the audiotape. Determine what you'll change. Listen for proper pace, volume and pauses.
- Assemble a friendly, small **audience** if possible.
- Give your **entire presentation** with visuals and equipment. Use the microphone and the videotape recorder if they're part of your presentation. Practice the best walking and positioning patterns for yourself so you'll miss tripping over cords. Tape cords to the floor. Speak to all of the empty seats. Practice your eye contact and eye movement around the room. Videotape this practice if possible.
- **Watch** your tape. Refine sections by practicing in front of a mirror.
- **Affirm** your strengths. Give yourself compliments and encouragement.
- **Visualize** yourself having successfully delivered the presentation. Bask in this feeling so you'll know how to reconstruct it during the real event!

The preparation phase of your presentation will make or break your meeting. To monitor your thoroughness, use this checklist of details. Your hard work during this phase will pay off!

Preparation Checklist

Meeting Date:_____ **Objective:**_____

Task	Completed/Not Necessary
	(X) (N/A)
Take *Self-Assessment Survey*	_____
Use *Four-P Needs Assessment*	_____
Prepare *Tentative Agenda*	_____
Complete *Meeting Plan*	_____
Complete *"Role Call"*	_____
Use *Personal Dimension Awareness Indicator*	_____
Complete *Audience Analysis Worksheet*	_____
Use *Needs Satisfaction Worksheet*	_____
Schedule *Communications Timeline*	_____
Send announcement memo	_____
Distribute *Survey Agenda*	_____
Prepare visuals and handouts	_____
Assemble actual agenda	_____
Develop presentation	_____
Review image tips	_____
Rehearse presentation	_____
Complete *Communications Timeline*	_____
State self-affirmation	_____

Part II:

Presentation

"If you don't strike oil in 20 minutes, stop boring."
Andrew Carnegie

 HAPTER 7

Documenting the Meeting

> "'They Say' the biggest liar in the world."
>
> *Paul Harvey*

After going to all of this trouble, it would be a shame to neglect a record of your successful meeting! Some meetings need more documentation than others, yet you'll want all of them recorded in some way. Your records prove that you've earned your paycheck by accomplishing your meeting objectives. Your records also show what decisions have been made by whom, as well as what actions have been taken. These records may be used as legal documents, so they must be accurate.

79

Five Ways to Record Meetings

- ## Notes

    ranging from an annotated agenda to traditional
    minutes writtten by an observer, such as a group
    secretary

- ## Annotated Visuals

    such as transparencies and flip charts, which are
    created during the meeting by the leader or other
    group representative

- ## Audiotape

- ## Videotape

- ## Transcription

    of every word said during the meeting

What method of documentation you select will depend
on your resources and needs. Usually, notes written by an
individual who represents the group are sufficient. The
amount of detail in the notes will vary depending on how
detail-oriented the note taker is. The leader and interested
participants can cue the note taker to include certain
statements and exclude others. If the meeting is short and
simple, a few notes under each agenda item will work. If
the meeting is more complicated, additional notes
identifying decision makers and topics of discussion
become more necessary. Agenda items, decisions and
actions provide the outline of the record. Taking notes is
easily affordable and doable. Paper, pen, patience, a
quick ear and a speedy hand are the only tools! If you
plan to enter the notes into a computer after the meeting is
over, consider having a computer in the meeting room

where the notes can be entered on the spot.

As you introduce more complex equipment into the recording process, you also introduce dependence on that equipment. Audio recorders and video cameras seem to wait for meetings to start before they refuse to work! This equipment is expensive, yet often available. If you decide to use equipment, provide backups and support personnel to cover breakdowns. Bring an extra tape, too. In addition, make sure someone in the group has paper and pencil – just in case!

Transcription is expensive. Someone must type a script of the meeting, identifying each speaker and recording each word. This is a tedious process reserved mostly for legal situations. The record actually takes more time to read than the group originally took to meet. The longer the record, the less likely people will want to review it. A long record also makes it more likely that people will not need to review it! It's certainly more difficult to dispute the accuracy of a tape or a transcript than it is handwritten notes. If you're unsure about how to record a meeting, ask the group to decide. Perhaps a combination of ways will be best.

In many cases you will be responsible for recording the meeting yourself. Ask for help in taking notes during discussions so that you can pace the meeting and participate as much as possible. Remember that you are also responsible for directing the content and the group dynamics. If the meeting is small and short, you can probably manage to record decisions and actions on your own agenda. Jot down key words to remind you later about important information to record. When you get back to your office and the computer, add your notes to your list of agenda questions. If you included an action plan format at the bottom of your agenda, that information is now a summary of the follow-up you'll need to do. An example of a format for actions and decisions is a fill-in statement such as this:

"WHO_____DOES WHAT_____BY WHEN_____"
    (name)   (action)   (date)

During the meeting, fill in the blanks with the dated plan and the names of those who agreed to complete them.

The **Minute System** categorizes more elaborate note taking at a larger and longer meeting. This system is divided into *before*, *during* and *after* tasks. *Before* the meeting begins, prepare the following items for the person who will assume the role of note taker.

Tools for the Note Taker

- A **list of people** expected to attend as participants, observers and leaders to ensure correct spelling and easy roll taking

- A **seating chart** marked with attendees' names to note group dynamics during the meeting and to credit comments to the correct source

- Three copies of the **current agenda**: one to write on, one for overflow and one to attach to the minutes when completed

- An accurate **timer or clock** that the group agrees to use, unless a timekeeper is present or the time does not need to be recorded

- **Recording equipment** and two tapes

- A **lined note pad** large enough for one of these two methods of note taking:
  1. *Column style*: Write notes in one column in the middle of the page or in either the left or right column, leaving space for additional information that may come out of sequence during the meeting.
  2. *Block style*: Write notes for separate agenda items on separate pages so that information can be added and categorized easily and clearly.

- Three or four **colored pens** to symbolize functions: red for decisions, green for actions, purple for discussion topics and black for other information

- Written copies of any **reports** to be presented

- Agreed **criteria** for what gets recorded and what is left out: names of those who move and second motions, discussion summaries, decisions and other details

- A recognizable **signal**, such as a raised hand or a surrender flag, that the recorder can use to call for a slowdown, a repetition or a clarification during the meeting

Now, we're ready for the meeting to start – on time, of course! The note taker will find this job easier to manage by using the **LAW** method:

> **L**isten first.
> **A**sk questions to get the needed answers recorded accurately.
> **W**rite fast.

Knowing what to write before dividing concentration between note taking and listening will improve accuracy. An audio recording of the meeting can be replayed for crucial wording in decisions.

Even *after* the meeting ends, several tasks remain. Type the minutes using agenda items as headings, and send them to members for their review before the next meeting. Only then is the meeting really over!

The LAW Method

*C*HAPTER 8

Arranging the Room

When two or more people agree to meet at a certain place at a specific time to interact in some way, a meeting results. Technology has expanded our ability to meet in unusual places at unusual times. Teleconferences, video conferences and computer-network conferences allow us to meet across town, country or globe without physically traveling outside our offices. Yet, we conduct most of our business through the traditional face-to-face meeting by gathering in the same room at the same hour. Understanding the characteristics of groups and interactions within groups will help you conduct effective meetings by achieving synergy, rather than wasting energy.

Characteristics of Groups

Two basic characteristics of groups are crucial for you to know:

- The **size** of the group influences your meeting management.

- The **attitudes** of the group influence seating choices.

Whether a group is small or large determines the time, space, equipment, approach and materials you'll need to run the meeting. Whether the group has a positive or a negative attitude toward its own composition and function, the leader, the topic and the task determines where participants seat themselves or where you seat them. Each of these key characteristics impacts how you arrange the room. Here's how your group's size and attitudes will affect your meeting:

- Size will determine how you label the group:

pair or dyad	=	*two members*
triad	=	*three members*
small group	=	*four to 15 members*
medium group	=	*16 to 25 members*
large group	=	*26 to 99 members*
huge group	=	*100 or more members*

- Size also determines what you can expect from a group. The **smaller** the group, the more options you have for a meeting place and time, the quicker the decisions the group will make, the less structure the meeting needs, the more personal and informal the discussion usually is, the more movement-oriented the interaction is and the more compliant the group usually is. The odd-numbered small group, usually

GROUP DYNAMICS:

Everyone talking at once.

composed of three to nine members, is best for
making fast decisions. Five to 11 members are good
for resolving problems. A small group is easier to
arrange in a circle, making each member visible and
audible to the entire group. Participation is usually
high in a small group.

- The **larger** the group, the more competitive subgroups are within the group. As the number of
participants increases in your meeting, consider
asking members to help as recorder, reporter or
timekeeper. Consider co-leaders for subgroups within
the large group. Each subgroup then acts similar to a
small group.

- People sit **closer** together when they meet in a large
room and have a positive perception of the leader.
Most Americans sit within three feet of another person
and stand an average of 18 inches apart. The more
motivated people are in a group, the closer they sit
together and the more often they say *we* instead of *I*.
But, if they sit together too closely too quickly, before
they've built rapport and trust, their attitudes tend to
be negative. Often, the people with the most positive
attitude about the meeting will sit close to the visual
displays and the leader. Speakers usually stand closer
to women than to men.

- People sit **farther** apart if they are independent,
unmotivated, disinterested, or feeling negative or
competitive. Those who are subordinates or superi-
ors to the other group members will also sit farther
apart than they would with their peers.

- Some members of a group, no matter the size, will
claim a spot in the meeting room and won't move
without resistance. If a member prefers one particular

seat, she or he may be resentful of intruders in the area. People who wear beepers may purposefully and thoughtfully claim a seat close to an exit to minimize the group's distraction. Others may sit where they can hear and see well. You may have to accommodate these claims when you shift among exercises in a meeting.

Where and with whom people sit in a meeting influences their participation and your preparation. As the physical and the psychological distances among members of a group decrease, motivation and interaction increase. Distances among members vary with time, combinations of people and the task. Your job is to monitor the distances!

Seating Arrangements

The location of doors, windows, aisles, visual displays and comfort centers, such as telephones, restrooms and refreshments, also affects interaction. Being aware of this will help you determine the best seating arrangement for your group. The seven most common arrangements are the *conference, U-shape, circle, pod, classroom, chevron* and *theater* styles. Each of these is diagrammed on the following pages.

Conference Style

visual display

leader

refreshments/displays

U-Shape Style

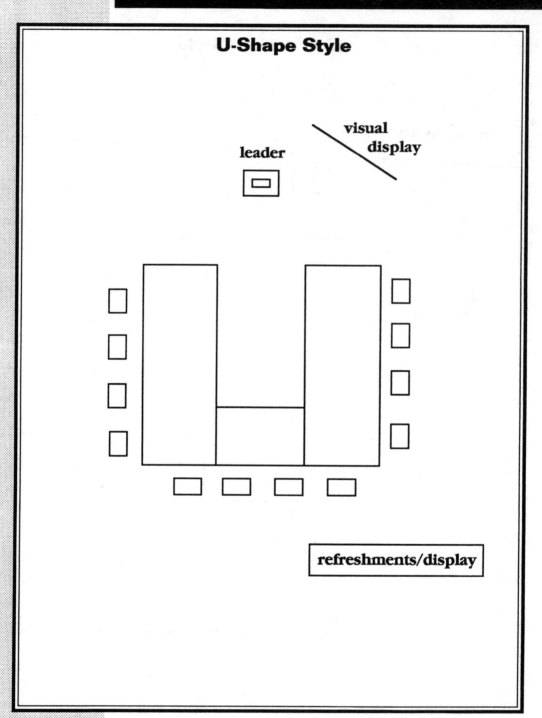

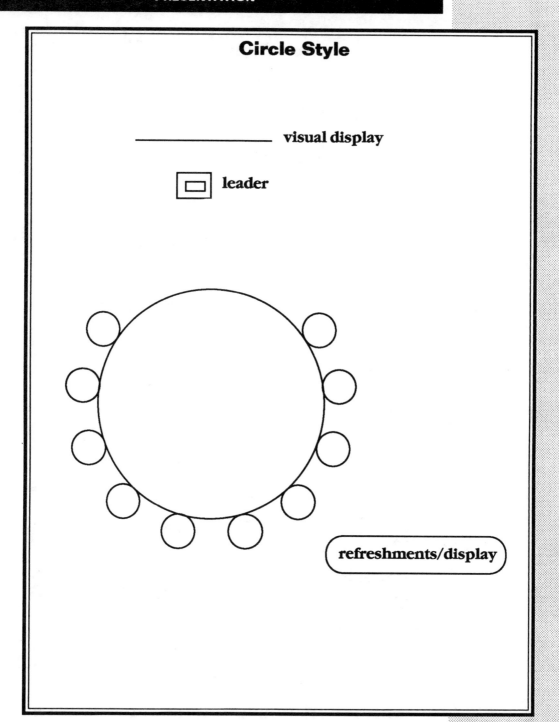

Pod Style

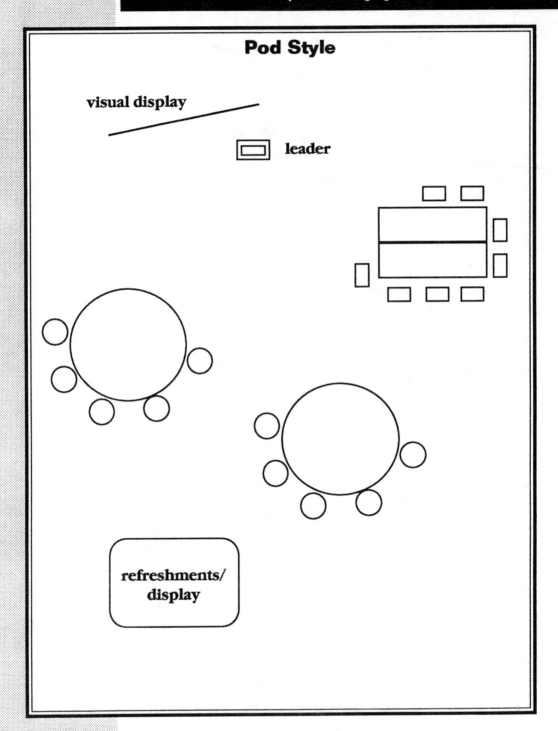

visual display

leader

refreshments/
display

Classroom Style

_____ visual display

☐ leader

refreshments/
display

Chevron Style

—————————— visual display

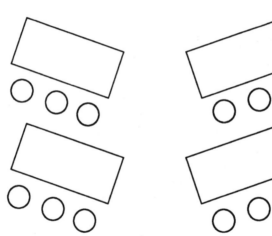 leader

refreshments/
display

Theater Style

visual display

leader

refreshments

display

The chart below will help you determine which arrangement to use for your meeting if you have some flexibility.

Seating Arrangement Chart

Style	Room Size	Group Size	Primary Function
Conference	Small	Small	Inform/ perform/ form
U-shape	Small/medium	Small	Inform/ form
Circle	Small/medium	Small/ medium	Inform/ form/ conform
Pod	Medium	Medium+	Form/ perform
Classroom	Medium	Large	Inform/ conform
Chevron	Medium+	Large	Inform/ conform
Theater	Large	Large	Inform/ conform

Each of these arrangements has its advantages and disadvantages. For example, if your room is small you can accommodate the conference, U-shape or circle styles for a group of four to 16 members. If the room is larger and you have portable chairs and tables, you have the most flexibility of style. If you're planning a work session, consider the pod and the conference styles. While all of the styles allow giving and getting information, the pod style is less comfortable and requires some movement of chairs for members to see any visuals or the speaker well. If tables are needed for writing during the meeting, avoid the theater and the circle styles. The chevron style is a variation of the classroom style. It staggers the members into diagonal rather than vertical rows to allow an unobstructed view of and from the podium.

Having a center aisle or two inside aisles allows convenient pathways in the classroom, chevron and theater styles for the speaker to move close to all members of the group. If the group is arranged in short rows, the two outside aisles may be enough. However the room is arranged, the speaker will want to be able to walk within a few feet of all the members. This allows everyone to hear and respond better. It's difficult to listen or to feel part of the group if the speaker is distant in either space or attitude.

Be thoughtful about any special needs of participants. These include ramps and wider aisles for wheelchairs, walkers and canes, front seating or an extra place next to the speaker for an interpreter for the hearing impaired, and back or aisle seating for those who must respond quickly to beepers and emergency calls. Consider your room arrangement carefully. The size of the room and the size and special needs of the group will impact the function and success of your meeting.

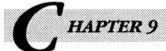

CHAPTER 9

Managing the Group

> "To manage men one ought to have a sharp mind in a velvet sheath."
>
> *George Eliot*

Meetings come in all sizes – from two to 20 to 200. You may need to meet with just one person to set or assess individual performance and development goals, to resolve a problem or eliminate an obstacle, to develop a relationship or to complete a plan of action. Each of these purposes requires making decisions. Your topic, timing, tactics and tact will influence these decisions and their outcomes.

The **SEES Confrontation Model** provides an effective strategy for a one-to-one meeting:

S   E   E   S

(signal)   (explanation)   (example)   (significance)

S

E

E

S

Meet in a place that is convenient and acceptable to both of you. You may need a place that is private if the nature of your meeting is to discuss individual performance. Perhaps meeting in one of your offices or at a restaurant would provide the appropriate environment. If the purpose of your meeting is comfortable for both of you, you may stand or sit. If your meeting is uncomfortable for one or both of you, sit together at the corner or along the side of a table. Avoid sitting across a table or desk from each other because that puts you in an adversarial position. Unlikely partners have worked together, including East and West Germany, America and Russia, and Apple Computer and IBM. If these larger concerns were able to come together, then surely it is possible to negotiate a smaller concern with Jerry or Chris! Begin with a **signal** that indicates your concern:

1. Use positive verbal and nonverbal language. Keep your posture open with your arms and legs uncrossed. This is a persuasive posture. For example, say, *"Thank you for meeting with me. Working together, we can make this situation productive."*

2. Ask for commitment. *"Will you work with me to resolve this situation?"*

Continue with an **explanation** of the situation:

3. Ask your partner to identify the problem or conflict. *"How do you understand the situation?"*

4. Listen without interruption.

5. Restate or paraphrase your partner's explanation until your partner says you understand it correctly. *"Do I understand correctly? You said..."*

Add a description of a specific and current **example** of the situation:

6. Clarify your view of this situation. Keep your view based on observation and avoid judgment or assumption. Make sure that your facts and interpretations are accurate and fair. Find something in your partner's statement to agree with. *"I agree that...and I see...differently.... For example,..."*

Conclude with the **significance** of the resolution:

7. State your expectations, the consequences and the effects.

8. Ask for agreement on the goal and its criteria. *Who* does *what* by *when?* If the process needs to be determined by both of you, discuss *how* it will happen. This agreement should be specific and realistic, positive and productive, measurable and dated.

9. Summarize the meeting and end positively and supportively. *"Thank you for your time and help. Your ideas will bring success. We'll meet next Tuesday at 10 a.m. in your office to review our action plan."*

> "In any argument, the man with the greater intelligence is always wrong, because he did not use his intelligence to avoid the argument in the first place."
>
> *Anon.*

The **SEES Confrontation Model** is a general strategy you can modify for any one-to-one meeting. A major cause of failed meetings is unresolved frustrations or fears. Frustration and fear result from needs that are not satisfied. Identifying the obstacles and working together to remove them and to empower one another will prevent, reduce or eliminate frustration or fear. People avoid confrontation because they fear something: losing someone's favor, losing their own temper, losing their anger or losing their indispensability. With every change, there's some distress. Yet, stress can paralyze or energize us.

Creative, constructive confrontation builds both confidence and competence. Without these, we're left with uncooperative, argumentative and, perhaps, aggressive co-workers – a situation that compounds frustration and fear. Four factors will help you use involvement and commitment to achieve your group's goals:

- organization skills
- conflict-resolution skills
- listening skills
- sense of humor

Each of these factors has roots in the **HIDDEN Agenda** discussed in Chapter 1. Most conflict results from differences in experiences or expectations. As the meeting leader, you are the pivot point for communication.

Where people sit in relation to one another affects their communication. You want communication to be open and constructive because you want a productive meeting.

What do you do when conflict arises? Conflict-resolution skills are essential for an effective leader in any meeting. Conflict gives us the opportunity to recognize other viewpoints and challenges us to be more creative in our thinking than we would otherwise. A meeting without conflict will end quickly with an acceptable result; a meeting with conflict may end later with a potentially better result. The following chart shows the **Seven C's**, the common behavioral styles for resolving conflict. Knowing the characteristics of these styles will help you determine what's most appropriate for directing your meeting and your audience.

Seven C's for Resolving Conflict

Method:	Conceal ......Control ......Compete......Compromise......Co-act......Collaborate......Concur

Approach:	[individual.................]	[group...]	[team..........................]

Demeanor:	(passive)	(assertive/ aggressive)	(assertive/ aggressive)	(passive/ assertive)	(passive/ aggressive)	(assertive)	(assertive)

Emphasis:	Conflict..Consensus

The individual decision-making process includes the conceal and control methods.

Conceal

To **conceal** means to deny a conflict or problem, to ignore it or to hope it will go away. Sometimes a miracle happens to change the situation so that you no longer have to deal with it, but usually this only postpones and intensifies the inevitable confrontation. Passive behavior often leads to unsatisfied needs and unsatisfactory results, allowing the conflict to remain without resolution.

Control

To **control** means that the individual takes charge of the decision-making process either by consulting with others or by dictating to them. This approach is most effective in managing a crisis, a severe time constraint or a routine decision, but least effective in managing almost any other kind of situation.

At the midpoint of the continuum, more than one person makes the decision or chooses the resolution.

Compete

To **compete** means that one group or coalition may achieve a goal while another group or coalition cannot. This is a desirable method only if you're on the winning side!

Compromise

To **compromise** means concessions or trades will get you part of what you want. This will happen if the goals are not mutual or if the methods used by the negotiating parties vary greatly. A mediator or an arbitrator will assist the group in reaching an understanding. The compromise is the middle ground between conflict (no agreement) and consensus (total agreement).

Co-act

To **co-act** means to cooperate but without complete cooperation. The goals may be mutual, but the expectations and experiences of the group are not shared. This method will benefit many members. To compete, to compromise and to co-act are group approaches to decision-making and problem-solving.

A group that agrees on a goal and how to accomplish it acts as a team. Team approaches to resolving conflict are the most enduring because they benefit the most members.

Collaborate

To **collaborate** means to work together in harmony to reach a decision. Many leaders appear during the meeting's discussion. Everyone agrees to support the final decision, although some may still have reservations.

Concur

To **concur** means that everyone agrees to the final decision without reservation. No peer pressure or lazy thinking causes this agreement. Each member of the team must be committed to the goal and to the team. Each member acts as your co-leader, who participates and communicates actively. Through conflict and chaos, a group becomes a team with a consensus.

Teams, synergy and consensus evolve gradually. They are ideals that can become real. Why do some groups become teams, yet others don't? What makes some groups achieve synergy while others waste everyone's time? How do some groups find consensus while others get stuck in compromise? Two diagrams will help explain the differences.

Individuals make up a group in this linear concept:

Person A + Person B + Person C + Person D = Group

Individuals also come together in this systemic concept, showing a team:

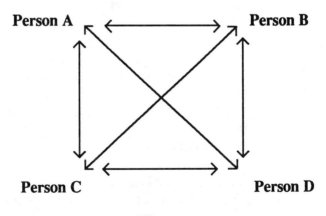

Team

This diagram shows that every team member interacts with every other team member. A group may be the sum of personalities as Person A interacts only with Person B, who interacts with Person C, and so on. But, a team has its own personality created through direct communication exchanges from each member to every other member. A team is connected and defined within itself. If the group is made up of dependent or independent individuals, the team is made up of interindependent individuals.

Team Leadership Skills

To focus your team during meetings to concentrate on the process and the objective rather than on the individual personalities, do three things:

- **Stay connected.** Communicate with each member and encourage all members to communicate directly with others. Stay in touch with dissenters and work toward resolution. Build a network.

- **Restate expectations.** Repeat and clarify what you will do, what you won't do, what you believe and what you think. Keep your values and your priorities well defined.

- **Be detached.** This sounds like a paradox, and it is! You will communicate better if you can distance yourself from any disagreement. Respond calmly. You may not like or understand a member's comment, but you may have to accept or acknowledge it. Keep an open mind.

The **Law of Combinations**, a systemic approach to group behavior, shows that relationships are powerful connections. For example, Sandy may be independent alone, dependent with Marge, belligerent with Nate and empowering with Mark. Sandy has the same personality, yet the connections differ. Sandy's interaction with each individual's personality traits causes a different reaction from Sandy. You see this in meetings all the time. Someone who usually works hard on one team slacks off when moved to another group. An overachiever in one place connects with an underachiever somewhere else.

The **Law of Combinations** explains why group dynamics change so often: as the combinations of people change, the relationships change. The group has a complex personality of its own. When the balance in that system changes, the meeting leader will experience resistance! Keeping balance within a meeting so that the group can become a team means paying attention to the combinations and communications.

An effective meeting facilitator knows a variety of strategies for encouraging members to participate and communicate, redirecting participation and communication when it's necessary. Discussion will go astray, the focus will dissolve, an interruption will occur, a person will dominate, an emotion will surface or something else will happen to stop the flow of your meeting. Three lists of strategies follow for preventing and reducing these unproductive situations. Use **Tips to Improve Listening**, **Tips to Increase Involvement** and **Tips to Transform Disagreement** to build consensus.

Listening

Listening is a fundamental communication skill, yet it is the most difficult skill to do well. Conducting a well-prepared meeting won't do you any good if the participants aren't listening to you or each other, or if you aren't listening to them! Everyone's attention will improve as listening improves. Use these tips to become a better listener. Then use these tips again to become a better speaker and leader in your meetings! Good listening saves both time and effort.

> Few of us know how to say nothing. Few of us know when.
> *Anon.*

Tips to Improve the Individual's Listening

- Listen with your **best ear**. Most people hear more effectively and efficiently through their left ears. Which ear do you use most often while talking on the telephone? Turn that ear toward your audience.

- Be **actively silent**. Speak only to clarify or summarize. Place a hand over your mouth if you have to!

- Identify **assumptions** you are making and avoid mind reading. Once a man saw another man moving a piano into a store. He offered to help. They pushed till they were exhausted. The store owner gasped, *"I can't believe this piano is so difficult to get out of here."* The stranger said, *"Out? Oh, no!"*

- Listen for the person's **transitions**, such as *"Another important point is...;" "For example,...;" "To further explain...."*

- Use **visualization** techniques to imagine what the speaker says. Create a mental movie of the message.

- **Connect** new ideas to information you already know, such as *"I can apply these tips for listening better to talking on the phone with clients."*

- **Restate** what the person just said before making your own comment.

- Tell yourself to **learn** something new from this person.

It's your task to focus your participants' attention. They will begin to listen better, comprehend more and remember longer when you use these tips.

Tips to Improve the Group's Listening

- Place yourself next to your listener's **left side** during a conversation or a presentation.
- Ask your listeners for their **attention**.
- Provide an **overview or outline** for your audience to follow. Listening increases when the ears and the eyes work together.
- Use attractive, simple **visual displays**.
- Tell your listeners how they'll **benefit** from the meeting, such as *"This information will save you time."*
- Use clear, concrete **transitions**.
- **Associate** new information with knowledge your audience already has.
- Whisper. Vary the **volume** of your voice.
- Speed up or slow down. Vary the **pace** of your speech.
- **Stop** talking.
- Use a **microphone** if your group's size is medium to huge.
- **Ask** those who can hear you to do something, such as *"If you can hear me, stomp your foot"* or *"Say 'yes' twice."* Other members will quiet down to find out what's going on!
- Give the group a **break**.
- Make or do something unusual, yet relevant to your point. **Surprise** to energize! Make a paper airplane if you're talking about travel expenses, stand on a table if you're talking about raising profits or draw a chalk line on the floor if you're talking about the bottom line.
- **Promise** to keep the meeting short and then keep your promise. It's easier to listen for a few, finite minutes than for an eternity.
- **Smile or laugh**, then relate something humorous to make your point.
- **Move** to keep your audience focused. Point to visuals, walk toward talkers and use wide gestures to maintain attention.
- Eliminate outside **distractions**, such as phones ringing and beepers sounding in the meeting room. Hold the calls and deactivate the beepers. If people need beepers, ask them to sit close to the exit, or check them at the door and have one person monitor them.
- Provide a comfortable **temperature** and straight-backed chairs for your audience. Cool air and erect **posture** promote good listening skills.
- Increase your audience's **involvement** in the meeting.

Involvement

Before you can involve people in making decisions and setting action plans in your meeting, you must get them to listen. Most will automatically get involved then. However, some may be unmotivated still. Your meeting goes nowhere without their participation and commitment. Once participants become part of the process for achieving the meeting's objective, the meeting will run smoothly and quickly. Here are some ideas to get you and your group started.

LISTENING

Two men were walking along a crowded sidewalk in a downtown business area. Suddenly one exclaimed: "Listen to the lovely sound of that cricket." But the other could not hear. He asked his companion how he could detect the sound of a cricket amid the din of people and traffic. The first man, who was a zoologist, had trained himself to listen to the voices of nature. But he didn't explain. He simply took a coin out of his pocket and dropped it to the sidewalk, whereupon a dozen people began to look around them. "We hear," he said, "what we listen for."

Kermit L. Long

Tips to Increase Involvement

- Ask the group to identify its **needs**. Have group representatives record them on a display, such as cork board, a marker board or a flip chart.

- Ask your audience to **do** something with the information they have, such as *"Check two items on this list that you think are top priorities."*

- Tell a **story**. People get involved in stories, especially if you ask them to imagine themselves in the situation you describe. *"Imagine you are just beginning this job. It's your first day here, and..."* Each member of the audience then becomes the lead character in your story. Remember that your story should illustrate a point that is pertinent to the meeting's objective.

- Encourage the group to share **leadership**. Ask for a volunteer to lead the small group discussion. That leader then asks someone else to lead the work session.

- Call someone by **name** and invite that person to comment. Plan this by inserting a signal in your presentation notes to ask Alice or Zack about this topic or point. Ask someone who has not commented yet to offer an opinion.

- Ask someone to **summarize** what has happened in the meeting so far.

- Invite participants to give **options** rather than advice. *"Have you thought of..."* works better than *"I think you ought to...."*

- Ask members of small groups to **stand** along a wall or beside their chairs when they complete a task. This allows members to move and encourages them to finish the task quickly.

- Build in **reflection** time. Pause with soft music playing in the background while participants record their thoughts. The music discourages talking and encourages thinking.

- Recognize **emotions** and body language. If Tony's head shakes, say, *"Tony, you're shaking your head. Would you share what you're thinking with us?"*

- **Ask** whether the group has any questions, concerns or suggestions.

- Ask the group to determine the best **action plan**, including specific tasks, people responsible for the completion of tasks and the time frame for the tasks.

- Focus on **mutual gain** so that everyone feels like a winner. Find a way to demonstrate how your audience will gain from each meeting you lead.

Disagreement

Differences of opinion, misunderstandings and mismatched priorities can cause friction any time people come together to talk. A good meeting leader will be firm, direct and flexible in the face of conflict. Your confident manner and a strong HIDDEN Agenda will lead participants toward the consensus side of the conflict-resolution continuum.

Tips to Transform Disagreement

- Use **humor** to defuse tension. The capacity to be playful gives you the psychological distance you need to remain calm and responsive without being reactive during meetings. A spontaneous laugh can offer the fresh perspective your group needs.

- Find a way to **agree**. Find something in the other argument or comment that you can agree with at least partially. *"I agree that this is an unfortunate situation, and I would remedy it differently than you have described."*

- Use **and** instead of *but*. *"We lowered our cost per unit by 3 percent and we must lower it another 4 percent by July 1."* Note that using *but* in that sentence would have discounted the original accomplishment.

- If someone from the audience verbally attacks you, **thank** that person for the comment or the concern, break eye contact and either proceed to your next point or ask the audience to respond. Avoid getting into a shouting match or a verbal duel. Even if you win the argument, you lose your audience's confidence that you can lead the group objectively.

continued

Tips to Transform Disagreement

- When telling bad news, use *I* or *we* as if you **"own"** it. When telling good news, say *you* as if they "own" it.

- Use **peer pressure** to keep divergent comments to a minimum. Ask the group early in the discussion to remind one another to stay on the topic. Identify a signal that members can use to suggest the speaker get back to the point at hand.

- Ask the group to **verify** any gossip or interpretations that appear in the meeting in order to avoid perpetuating rumors or assumptions. *"How do you know that?"*

- Avoid **triangling**, complaining about a person who is not part of the conversation. This tactic leads to misunderstandings, secrets and mistrust every time! Speak directly to a person if you want a conflict resolved.

- **Restate** a person's disagreement and ask if you understand it correctly. Be sure you hear what that person is saying and that the person feels you are taking the disagreement seriously.

- Ask the person who disagrees if she or he wants it stated in the **record** of the meeting or ask if the point is appropriate for the next meeting's agenda. Delaying or rescheduling such points will often defuse them. With time between this meeting and the next, some of the points will resolve themselves.

- If a person who is hostile toward you or the group must be in the meeting, seat that person to your side – the amicable **position** – and not across from you – the antagonistic position.

- Focus on **current** issues – the here and the now. You can't change the past; you can change how you respond to the present and to the future.

- Focus on the **behavior** and the **issue**, not the person. If someone calls you "incompetent," reply, *"I hear your frustration that this matter is not resolved yet. Work with me, and together we'll find a solution."*

continued

113

Tips to Transform Disagreement

- Use a **mediator** or an **arbitrator**. Ask the dissenting parties to agree to abide by the outcome that will be facilitated or decided by a person they mutually appoint.
- Describe **observations** in nonthreatening, nonjudgmental language. *"You claim that..."* suggests that the person is lying. A more neutral response is *"Is my understanding correct? Are you saying that...?"* Saying *"Your department never gets its annual report on time"* may be unfair. Perhaps the printer delayed the department's publication two of the last five years. Avoid making conclusions while describing situations.
- Use an *"I Message."* This is a direct, clear, assertive and non-threatening statement that allows the speaker to describe personal feelings, observations and perceptions in a specific situation. Four parts of this message work together to form a complete communication about a current situation: *observation, emotion, impact* and *action*.

  "When I receive a report late *(observation),* I feel flustered *(emotion).* Then I don't have the time to do as good a job as I'd like to and as my supervisor would like me to do *(impact).* Please make a realistic deadline for your staff so that we can all count on the scheduled completion of an excellent project *(action)."*

  The *"I Message"* says *"This is how I understand the situation, how I feel about it, what happens, and what I want you or me to do about it to keep it from happening again."*

- Use the *FOCUS* model to transform complaints that are not negotiable into targets that are. Individuals or teams can use this process:

What are your **f**eelings about the situation?	*I feel...*
What are your **o**bjections or concerns?	*I am frustrated that...*
What are the **c**onsequences?	*I worry that...*
What would **u**topia be?	*I wish...*
What **s**atisfaction are you looking for?	*I want...*

If you use these tips to manage your group, you will have a successful meeting!

CHAPTER 10

Opening the Meeting

> "My way is to begin with the beginning."
> *Don Juan*

Going into surgery, writing a speech, asking someone for a date, buying a car or taking a new job – each causes stress, each involves risk and each offers the chance of something better. Typically, the hardest or scariest part of anything is the beginning. Each beginning signals a change, and change is a step toward a potential transformation. Each meeting provides opportunities for each participant to become better in some way.

Not everyone welcomes this chance. You, however, are in a unique position to ease the anxiety felt just before a meeting begins and during its first few minutes. Your leadership will set the tone for the meeting. You have already gone a long way toward making the meeting a valuable experience for everyone by preparing the *content* – including objectives, materials and participants – and part of the *context* – including group dynamics, seating arrangements and special considerations for those participants with physical or schedule constraints. Yet, before you can effectively direct a meeting, you must host the members. Hosting means further developing the context of the meeting during the greeting and the opening. You can expect the initial minutes of the gathering to include greeting participants as they arrive and the three elements of the opening:

- *introductions* of key presenters
- *acceptance* of the purpose and the schedule
- *instructions* or recommendations for direction

How can you make yourself and others more comfortable as you ease into the content of the meeting? Suggestions follow.

Ways to Reduce Anxiety

You present yourself as well as the content of a meeting. Realizing that others are making judgments about you and the presentation may make you nervous. Perhaps speaking in front of a group makes you even more nervous. Here are some tips to help you compose yourself, so you'll think and speak clearly.

- *Preparation*: Do as much as you can before the meeting day to get ready. Use the checklists in this book to keep yourself organized. Review the material an hour before the meeting and then relax. Trust your preparation.

- *Breathing*: Relax with a few deep breaths before you begin greeting people. Pause during a conversation or a presentation just long enough to talk yourself into being calm, collected and clear. Breathe to a count of ten: "1, 2, 3, 4" as you inhale and "5, 6, 7, 8, 9, 10" as you silently exhale.

"Worry affects circulation, the heart and the glands, the whole nervous system, and profoundly affects the heart. I have never known a man who died from overwork, but many who died from doubt."

Dr. Charles Mayo

- *Affirmations*: Write down your strengths and your positive expectations for your performance during the meeting. Say these aloud. Avoid any negative thoughts. Restate your affirmations with commitment, conviction and confidence. Decide to be successful!

- *Visuals*: Use visuals such as transparencies or flip charts as presentation cues for yourself as well as aids for your audience. Once in sequence, these materials provide an outline of your content to help you keep on track and on time. You may want to make notes for yourself, too. Use a sticky note that you can quickly read and peel off a transparency as a reminder to ask a question, clarify a term or pause for effect. Use lightly penciled notes that only you can see and read on a flip chart prepared for the audience.

- *Movement*: Use your body to communicate. Use your face, your arms and your legs; smile, gesture and walk. The exercise will relax you by consuming your nervous energy and giving it a productive outlet.

- *Delegation*: Ask others to do as much of the preparation and presentation as possible. Ask someone else to give a report, to facilitate a work group or to photocopy materials. You have to coordinate this process, but you don't have to do it all by yourself! Invite others to develop their leadership skills along with you.

- *Discussion*: Rely on discussion to help you when someone asks a question you don't have an answer for or when someone says something hostile to you. Open the response to your audience, either an individual or the whole group. You may say: *"I'm not sure how to respond to that. Perhaps some of you* (extend your arm toward the audience) *have helpful comments."*

- *Visualization:* Imagine yourself successfully conducting the meeting. Review the elements of the meeting and what you plan to say and do during each. See yourself looking attractive, sounding articulate, moving with poise and feeling good! Visualize what a good meeting looks like and place yourself in it.

You'll want to clarify your expectations and ready your audience for active listening and enthusiastic involvement during the meeting. An anxious audience has its guard up and its mind closed. To increase collaboration in achieving the meeting's objective, identify your audience's concerns.

Ways to Reduce Your Audience's Anxiety:

- *Preparation:* Your audience will appreciate having everything in position and ready to go. It shows that you value their time. Besides, they base their perception of your competence on your preparation.

- *Greetings:* Meet participants at the door as they arrive. Address each by name if possible, or introduce yourself. If there are too many new people for you to remember everyone's name, ask the participants to wear name tags. Offer a positive, sincere comment such as *"Thank you for being here today"* or *"Did you enjoy your vacation on the coast?"* to recognize each person. Learn names to gain positive attitudes.

- *Promise:* Make a promise to keep on the accepted schedule and topics. Everyone will appreciate your commitment to finish the agenda within the agreed time frame.

- *Humor:* Project a pertinent cartoon or a brief story on the wall for your audience to see when they arrive for the meeting. This will entertain them, give them a discussion piece and encourage them to arrive early next time because they realize you reward their efforts to be on time.

- *Music:* Play soft, instrumental music to encourage participants to relax prior to the meeting or to internalize information and reflect on applications for new knowledge during the meeting. Music facilitates creative problem-solving and is a great transitional activity between the "outside world" and the "meeting world" or between information and formation segments of the same meeting. It adds a positive dynamic to the mood of a meeting. It also provides a chance for individuals to collect their thoughts prior to group work, thus facilitating the group goal.

- *Sharing:* Recognize the sacrifices people have made to attend the meeting. Some may have worries that will interfere with their attention during the meeting. Share updates about participants' lives, concerns and pleasures at the start of the meeting to build personal relationships. After all, it is people who create teams and teams that solve problems. If you're afraid your car won't start after the meeting is over, concentrating on the meeting will be difficult. During a sharing time, however, someone will volunteer to drive you back to your office or your home. Some meeting leaders list this time of "comfort and caring," "joys and sorrows" or "sharing and caring" as the first item on their agendas.

- *Movement:* Encourage participants to move around during a networking time or an opening activity. Ideas for how to do this will come later in the chapter. You'll want to get everyone's minds and bodies working toward more complete commitment to the agenda. The physical activity will activate the mental activity. Exercise activates imagination!

- *Stories*: All great meetings include an anecdote, a simulation or an illustration to make a point. The laughter or other emotional responses break down attention barriers that people carry into meetings. People bond with stories, and bonding reduces anxiety.

Ways to Open a Meeting

The opening of a meeting is the opening of minds. Consequently, how you begin a meeting is the most important part of your strategy. *What* a person says may not be as important as *how* it is said. The emphasis on certain words or on certain meanings can change the message of a statement. Practice emphasizing the following underlined words: *You will improve, You will improve,* and *You will improve*. All send different messages. To help you set the stage for a successful meeting and to build a sense of community among the participants, use any of the following ideas or allow them to spark other possibilities.

- Begin with an inspirational **quotation**, a stimulating testimonial or a startling statistic to create interest.

- Using your company's values or action priorities, label signs with key words that represent them. Post them on the walls in separate locations around the room and invite participants to **take a stand** under the one they think is most important now.

- Have participants identify **topics** that need discussion. Write them on sticky notes and post them in an appropriate column on a flip chart. Columns can be labeled *yes/no, now/later, 1-2-3* or some other way.

- Display a timeline or other **overview** of the current project.

- Compare your **perception** with the participants' perceptions of how they will gain from this meeting.

- Use **props**, music, a song, a slide show, a video, a story, a skit or a trick to capture interest. Juggle apples and oranges to show how your company must juggle its priorities in order to maintain a healthy operation. Toss a ball to a participant and have that person ask a question or make a statement regarding the objective for the meeting. Once done, that participant throws the ball to someone else to add another thought. Bring in an umbrella or a children's plastic wading pool to illustrate umbrella operations or pooling together. Dress up as Ben Franklin to make a point about diplomacy and invention in a global market. Read a children's story to illustrate a quality. Use your imagination to capture the participants' imaginations.

- Use a **forced analogy** to stimulate creative thinking. *"How is our service or product like an animal, a snack, an automobile or a candle?"*

- Add the number of **years** of working experience each participant has and announce the total. Add their ages minus the number of participants to find the total number of years of communication experience. Build confidence that with the sum of their experience, participants will successfully face the main issue presented in the meeting.

- Post butcher paper along one wall of the room. Invite each participant to **draw or write** one thing that contributes to the total vision of the group. This creative brainstorming technique gets people and ideas moving.

- Each participant selects a numbered playing **card** from a basket and must contribute during the meeting at least the number of times shown on the card.

- Make a **promise** at the beginning of the meeting to end on time.

- Record each current problem, concern or conflict on a separate sheet of paper. Wad each into a ball or make each into a paper **airplane**. Sail one at a time to a participant. Team up participants to list possible resolutions and later report them to the entire group.

- **Refer** to the last meeting's conclusion, either its decisions or its closing exercise. Tie in the opening for this meeting with the end of the last one.

- Use the following lists of tips to make unusual **introductions** of leaders and participants and to give clear, concise **instructions**. Both techniques will grab your audience's attention.

Introductions

If you're introducing a superior or a speaker, you'll want to ensure the audience's attention and appreciation during the presentation. This is a matter of professional courtesy. Besides, if someone else is doing the presenting, you get to relax and that deserves proper acknowledgment!

Tips for Making Introductions

- Take a **sip** of water and then **pause** before introducing yourself or others. Lubricate your throat and collect your thoughts.

- Make an important introduction approximately five minutes into the opening. Set the context for your participants by identifying reasons and ways to remember this person. People remember a **name** better after they have information and a face to associate the name with.

- Provide participants with written **biographies** of main presenters. Photographs posted on a bulletin board are also helpful.

- List significant **life experiences** of a guest speaker on a transparency and project it during the introduction. Include information your guest supplies such as ancestral background, unusual non-career jobs, family members' occupations or interests, hobbies and personal successes. For example, introduce a speaker as *"a member of a family that owns a crafts business, one of nine children who has one child, a former clam digger, an expert sandwich chef, a frustrated volleyball enthusiast, a Cherokee-Ukrainian-American and a student of tightrope walking."*

- Give participants **three minutes** to discover something unusual about a partner or something good that happened to them that week. Use the information to introduce each other to the group.

- Ask each participant to sign in on a **transparency** projected on the wall. Each then states an expectation for the meeting. Once the names are recorded, the group could analyze the handwriting!

- If you have a large, diverse group, ask people to stand or to raise hands in response to interesting **questions** such as *"How many of you have attended a meeting already today?"* or *"How many of you were born in this state?"* or *"How many of you remember when this company was first established?"* Make sequential statements such as *"Stand if you have worked here for at least two years. Remain standing if you've been here for five years...for ten years...."* Those who feel protective of their privacy may, of course, silently refrain from participating.

Tips for Giving Instructions

Much time is wasted in meetings due to inadequate instructions. Frustration mounts when people don't know what to do or how to do it. People will judge your entire preparation on how you give directions. Build their confidence in you and save time by stating clear, concise instructions the first time.

- Ask participants to do only **three or fewer** tasks in sequence. People get more confused as you add tasks because they begin thinking about or doing the first while you're describing the last. Keep instructions simple for best results, or be prepared to explain them again!

- Give **both** spoken and written instructions for clarity and reference.

- Tie in the instructions to the **rationale** or the desired **results**. Show how what you're asking the participants to do will impact the objective of the meeting.

- Ask for **questions** and be ready to clarify any directions you've given.

All of these ideas are effective openers. Remember that the opener is actually the first transition in your meeting, the one between the outer world of daily activity and the inner world of the meeting. Some of these ideas may also be effective transitions between activities and agenda items during the meeting. They encourage and maintain enthusiasm.

You will begin at the scheduled time, but experienced leaders caution you to begin with an item or activity of interest, yet one that is not the most essential. This accommodates late arrivals, while acknowledging those participants who have arrived on time. It also acts as a warm-up for the real task ahead. Usually, the most effective sequence of elements is opener first, then introductions and instructions last. Creating movement and excitement during the opening moments will ensure a good meeting. Now you're ready to deliver the content.

*C*HAPTER 11

Delivering the Content

> "If you have an important point to make, don't try to be subtle or clever. Use a pile-driver. Hit the point once. Then come back and hit it again. Then hit it a third time – a tremendous whack."
>
> *Winston Churchill*

This is your big moment – the substance of your meeting. You have drawn on many resources to get to this point, and you can be confident that you are well prepared. If your palms moisten, your voice cracks and your knees buckle just a little, this chapter will dry your palms, even your voice and straighten your knees! You'll learn proven training strategies and trust-building techniques that will increase your credibility with your audience. Members will trust your experience and your expertise. They will perceive you as a leader who has something significant to say.

You'll learn about the **Six Effective Training Strategies** in this chapter.

Prophecy Effect	**Leapfrog Effect**
Reward Effect	**Simmer Effect**
Memory Effect	**Spiral Effect**

Six Effective Training Strategies

Prophecy Effect

You get what you expect! Positive-thinking techniques such as visualization and affirmations help people prepare for success and recognize that failure leads to future success. Ashleigh Brilliant, the humorist, says, "Watch out! It's quite possible that some of my best mistakes haven't yet been made." Keeping an open, optimistic mind is essential for anyone who wants to learn. Removing frustrations and other obstacles to success will help you serve the participants better, freeing them to learn information more efficiently and to apply it more creatively. Post some of these reminders in your meeting room and display them on your meeting memos and materials:

Blame = Lame Aim   *Failure = Unborn Success*
Dare to Share   *Inherent Merit*
Evolve Excellence   *Pessimism is a Pest*
Smile Style   *Optimism = My Option*

Leapfrog Effect

This discussion technique allows a topic to move onto a short tangent that is then directed back to the main point. Each jump provides additional information or experience that rounds out participants' knowledge. A leader can begin this technique by getting agreement on the purpose and objective of the meeting. The leader then introduces the first agenda item and encourages discussion. If the talk deviates too much from the original item, the leader asks or shows how the current statements are pertinent to the objective. After this item circles back to the main point, the next agenda item is discussed. You may want to invite participants to monitor the discussion leader or any contributor by asking how the current discussion is relevant to the task at hand. They may want to use a horn, a bell or a flag to signal a return to the main point or a rationale for continuing on the present tangent. To have an effective meeting, you must assure the participants that discussions stay on track, that participants' time and experiences are valued and that they have some control over the direction and scope of the discussion. This will encourage creative problem-solving that would not be as obvious without the short, redirected tangents. At the same time, misdirected or nondirected tangents are discouraged and speakers are held accountable by the group. This technique also provides closure as discussion is completed. People leave a meeting knowing exactly *what* is expected of *whom* by *when* because all of the short tangents are centered on the original objective.

Reward Effect

People respond favorably and loyally when they feel they and their time are valued. Recognizing work, feelings and outcomes is essential in building teams and trust. Rewards may be spontaneous and intangible such as laughs, fun or applause, or they may be formal and tangible such as published accolades, plaques or promotions. A seemingly insignificant mint at each participant's place at an after-lunch meeting or a word of thanks during the opening of a meeting can make a significant impact on the morale of a group or an individual.

Simmer Effect

Change takes time. Sometimes ideas need to cook to unlock their full aroma and flavor. A wise proverb says when a person is ready to learn, the teacher will appear. Learning to read, to play the piano or to ride a bicycle takes mental and physical readiness. So does good business. Your timing is often crucial in gaining and holding the market share. You are providing a service to the participants in the meeting by conducting it. Your readiness has a direct impact on their readiness to achieve the objective. As important as being prepared is being flexible so that you can take advantage of the natural timing of a point of interest. When vision and values align, readiness should result in action. Your task is to align as many factors as possible and to ready the group to take action. Readiness means matching the *will* with the *skill*, the *desire* with the *design*.

If you have a suggestion for a new way to handle a situation – perhaps an innovative customer service plan or a new computer system – mention it as a possibility, allow time to pass, mention it as a probability, allow more time to pass and then mention it as a reality. Once people are comfortable with the idea and it's not new anymore, they'll consider it more seriously than they would have originally.

This also works when creating ideas. Ideas sometimes take time to grow out of a general concept into a specific strategic plan or a new or unusual product line. Allow percolation time when setting time frames. Allow for a few unstructured minutes in each meeting schedule to accommodate the extra time needed to percolate ideas. Your preparation, their readiness and a flexible strategy will collide in a creative burst. Freeing their imaginations will reduce stress-caused illnesses and refresh stale minds.

Memory Effect

Conducting or attending a meeting means remembering a lot of material. The memory-effect method gives you a system for learning information you want to present and for presenting information you want your audience to know, connecting the new knowledge with familiar information and pacing repetitions to ensure retention. Use the **Seven R's** when you rehearse a presentation and use them again when you instruct participants in a meeting.

Seven R's to Remember

Relax. Prepare your audience members' minds for the new information by providing a relaxed atmosphere with music, humor or exercise. Release

the tedium and the tension as much as possible
before the agenda begins.

- *Reflect*: Have your audience think about the objective
  before the meeting or as an opener to it.

- *Read*: See the new material. Visuals are useful.

- *Recite*: Say the new information. Small group
  interaction works well.

- *Record*: Write or draw the new information.
  Worksheets and group projects work for this
  technique.

- *Respond*: Interpret and critique the new information
  as it relates to old information. Make mental
  associations between the new and the old knowledge
  to cement them in your memory. Analyze and apply
  unfamiliar concepts to familiar situations to remember
  them more easily. Discussions and projects work
  well.

- *Review*: Several of these steps are repetitious. By
  repeating something new, the brain forges it into
  long-term memory so that it can be retrieved next
  week. Do you remember cramming for a test in
  school, learning the information just long enough to
  finish the test? Without relying on repetition and
  review, few of us could pass any of our high school
  final exams now!

Spiral Effect

The sixth strategy for delivering the content of a
meeting offers an audience the chance to build experience
and knowledge into a desired result. Each step moves
toward the meeting goal just as each rung of a spiral
staircase leads toward the top. Each step within the
overall design of your meeting should have a purpose.

Some steps must build on earlier steps. If your material is sequential, this strategy will help you organize and present it in a form that your audience can easily grasp. Using a visual or the metaphor of the spiral staircase will help you explain the relationships between the steps.

The **Brainstorm Spiral** shows this strategy in action. Brainstorming creates alternatives within the decision-making and problem-solving processes. Use this model during your meeting to generate discussion and action. The tools you'll need include a timer or alarm clock, a pen or marker and a visual display. The roles are the leader, the recorder, the timekeeper and the thinkers.

Brainstorm Spiral

Planning:

- Select the brainstorming team – usually two to 12 people – and choose roles. *Create synergy.*
- Agree on the goal and the time frame – usually 15 minutes or less. *Focus on consensus.*

Listing:

- Close the critical mind and open the creative mind. *Invite surprises.*
- Call out ideas and accept them all as possibilities. *Be spontaneous.*
- Record all ideas in their original language and order. *Write fast.*
- Finish within the allotted time. *Race the clock.*

Discussing:

- Renegotiate the time frame with the team or proceed to the next step. *End or add to the list.*
- List all of the influencing factors surrounding your ultimate decision: money, travel, location,

> "You cannot teach a man anything; you can only help him to find it within himself."
> *Galileo*

personnel, time, equipment, space and ethics.
Study the context.

- Review the list of ideas with a critical mind, identifying the probable outcomes of each option. *Challenge your limits.*

Deciding:

- Highlight the favored options. *Vote with vision.*
- Establish the criteria for selecting the best option. *Be clear.*
- Revise your favored options to suit your situation. *Test the possibilities.*
- Select the best option. *Take charge of change.*
- *Follow through and review.*

Whatever training strategies you use, you must keep track of the timing and the content. The timing should match the expected life cycle or energy flow of the meeting. Because you can't maintain a constant peak for attention during most meetings, you'll plan when you want to peak your participants' interest. If you're motivating your sales force, you'll want to build to a tall peak at the end of the meeting. If you're instructing, you'll plan several peaks throughout the meeting.

Visuals

The mind can read a picture faster than it can understand the words. Your audience will appreciate the visual displays you prepare for focusing ideas. The **Visual Display Chart** on the next page provides recommendations for the use of visuals. Keep all displays simple, clear and visible. Use headings and bullets when appropriate.

Visual Display Chart

Visual	Group Size	Recommendations
Handouts	All sizes	Mail them early as background material; place them at seats if they're needed during the meeting; distribute them at the door as people leave; include instructions and sources; check page sequence; color-code multiple handouts for easy reference
Overhead transparencies	Medium to large	Use 25 words and six lines or less on the horizontal side; use 24-point type or 1/4-inch high letters; use one or two type styles and three or fewer colors; use temporary ink; keep an extra lamp and extension cord handy; use the click sound of the machine to focus your audience's attention
Slides	All sizes	Test for accurate position of slides to ensure right-side-up displays; see tips for transparencies; keep display to 25 minutes or less; keep illustrations simple and clear
Videotapes	Small to medium	Use a 25-inch or larger monitor screen; preset video in proper position and check tracking; show 25 minutes or less
Flip charts/ Marker Boards	Small	No more than eight lines vertically; use 2- to 4-inch letters with 2-inch leading between rows; no more than 20 words; two blank pages between each pair of prepared flips; index flips on one side with a sticky name tag that you can write on and hold; elevate displays for larger groups; use dark ink

Ways to Increase Your Credibility

Every segment of every chapter you've read in this book so far will enhance your credibility. How believable and trustworthy you are depends on your audience's perception of your confidence, commitment and competence. If your audience members don't perceive these qualities, they will withhold their attention and their commitment. You may be honest, caring and skilled, but if your audience doesn't *think* you are, you're sunk! Review this list of ideas, checking any that you intend to use during your next meeting.

Ways to Increase Your Credibility

____ Start meetings on time.

____ Be well prepared.

____ Make your answers short and direct.

____ Use concrete, colorful comparisons.

____ Use strong action verbs.

____ Give specific examples.

____ Define terms, problems and instructions.

____ Avoid frequent blinking.

____ Avoid answering an inappropriate question by directing a question back to the questioner.

____ Think before you speak.

____ Keep the discussion in control and focused.

____ Listen without interrupting, and keep a list of key words each speaker says to keep track of the discussion.

____ Check interpretations of people's statements for accuracy and clarification.

____ Restate your understanding of a statement and ask for clarification.

____ Summarize periodically to highlight significant points.

____ Identify consequences of each decision.

____ Facilitate the plan for action.

____ Establish a clear time limit and end on time.

____ Acknowledge the value or truth of comments even if you do not agree with them.

continued

Ways to Increase Your Credibility

___ Ask the quiet participant for a comment or an opinion.

___ Make direct eye contact with those who are speaking.

___ Break eye contact and redirect the discussion if someone is dominating the talk.

___ Remain calm, even if someone is hostile toward you.

___ Ask someone who is dominating the discussion by repeating a point over and over to record a statement for the minutes or write it on a flip chart. That way, everyone is sure it is physically recorded and mentally noted.

___ Ask the group to verify information.

___ Use people's names when you address them.

___ Defuse any verbal attacks on or toward any participant.

___ Tell the truth without exaggeration, sarcasm, ridicule or excuse.

___ Walk among the participants rather than hide behind a lectern or a table.

___ Check your facial and body expressions to make sure they're consistent with your words.

___ Avoid upward inflections that make your statements sound like questions.

___ Check your tone, pitch and volume.

___ Avoid disclaimers such as *I may be wrong* and tags such as *don't you?*

___ Use multisensory language and activities.

___ Take ownership for your mistakes.

___ End on time.

continued

Your meeting is now under way, and you are delivering the content. You're conducting an effective, efficient meeting. Your participants are attentive and enthusiastic. And you are competent and confident!

You have now finished the most demanding phase of planning and conducting a meeting. The communication skills you used while speaking and listening to your team kept you focused on both the meeting objective and the process.

Presentation Checklist

Meeting Date:_____ Meeting Objective:_____

Task	Completed/Not Necessary
	(X) (N/A)
Arranged for documentation	_____
Prepared recorder's materials	_____
Made room accessible to all participants	_____
Arranged seats appropriately	_____
Reviewed group dynamics	_____
Reviewed tips for listening	_____
Reviewed tips for involving participants	_____
Reviewed tips for transforming disagreement	_____
Reviewed tips for reducing anxiety	_____
Planned the greeting	_____
Planned the opener	_____
Rehearsed the introductions	_____
Rehearsed the instructions	_____
Selected the delivery strategy	_____
Reviewed tips for increasing credibility	_____
Completed a successful presentation	_____

Part III:
Completion

"Strike while the iron is hot."

Proverb

C HAPTER 12

Finishing the Meeting

Once you've delivered the content, the hard part is over. What remains are the closing, the follow-through, the follow-up and the beginning of the next meeting. If you made a presentation during the meeting, you acted out a scene in the play. After reaching the climax of the content, you're back to the job of director. This chapter will show you how to complete one meeting and begin preparing for the next one.

Are you beginning to suspect that planning and conducting meetings are like cleaning your house and caring for your car – never-ending chores? Good business practices never end and neither do business meetings. However, you've made great strides toward the most productive meeting ever held by making it this far into the book! Your determination and dedication will drive you toward success!

You'll want participants to leave the meeting with a

positive sense of accomplishment and a renewed sense of commitment. For that to happen, the closing exercise must enlighten, entertain or both. Several ideas follow.

Ways to Close a Meeting

Finding closure allows your team a few minutes to assess the meeting objective one more time. Equally as important is acting as a community one more time. The rapport that develops after working together in this meeting will carry over until the next meeting. A closing exercise clears up any remaining confusion and opens up communication for the interim between meetings.

- **Summarize** or ask someone else to summarize the main points and decisions of the meeting.

- Distribute a brief **values survey** and promise to have the composite ready for the next meeting. Use the HIDDEN Agenda, for instance. Write the key words on a flip chart and ask each participant to rank the six items, high to low, on a 3-by-5 index card. Collect the cards in a tray beside the exit. Tally the rankings and list them on the chart for the next meeting. Use the results as a greeting or an opener. This is a team-building exercise because many will discuss personal and corporate values as they go out the door and when they return through that door for the next meeting.

- A **round-robin** activity in which each participant is asked to respond to the team gives everyone the center stage for at least one moment before adjournment. Here are a few ways to stimulate a round robin.
  - *Ask each member to say what she or he learned.* "I learned that this group thinks like a team!" "I learned a new way to approach the accounting department."

"I learned that working together is more fun and more productive."

- *Invite each participant to give a personal affirmation.*

  "I am capable."
  "I will complete all five miles of the Corporate Challenge Run!"

- *Invite each to give an appreciation for a team member.*

  "I appreciate Jack for asking me about my opinion today."
  "I appreciate Kay for pushing us to think of fresh options."

- *Ask each to commit to a task or an action.*

  "I'll help Janice get the rest of the data for the research report."

  "I'll call the head of public relations to get the publicity out on our project."
  After members make a statement, hand them a marker to record the commitment and the completion date on a visual display that will be used as a reference for the next meeting.

- *Ask each to give a one-word comment, thought or feeling.*

  "Glad."   "Excited."   "Surprised."   "Realistic."

- End with a brief **evaluation**, such as "What was the most helpful part of this meeting?" Ask each member to write a short answer on a sticky note or an index card to leave on or by the door on the way out.

- End with a **laugh**.

- Ask for a stand-up evaluation of the meeting: stand up to show a high level of effectiveness, remain seated for average and kneel for low level. The symbolism will probably get some laughs as everyone rises to exit!

- Ask everyone to stand, stretch for six seconds and clap four times. Then bow and say, "Thank you for that standing ovation!"

- Stop the timer or alarm. If you set the clock at the beginning of the meeting, it will either interrupt you at mid-sentence or your audience will be counting down the final 10 seconds!

After the Meeting

Network with individuals after the meeting. Use this valuable time to learn about others' lives, careers, skills, awards and preferences. These insights will prove helpful as you plan other meetings. **Thank** support personnel for their help in planning the meeting and presenters for their efforts in conducting the meeting. Thank yourself for a job well done by treating yourself to a token **reward**.

Within an hour after the meeting ends, while your impressions are still fresh, jot down observations to improve or include for the next meeting. Keep a **log** that includes your thoughts and feelings about your meetings: settings, participants, comments and any other information of interest. Record names of resource people, sketches of seating arrangements and training strategies that worked or didn't work, promises you or others made, descriptions of openers and closings, action plans with time frames and names of participants who voiced concerns you want to hear more about. Use your log to guide you in following through on commitments you've made to individuals or groups. This log will help you and the recorder fill in gaps in the **minutes**, improve communication with team members between meetings and remind you how much better your meetings are getting each time. The log will also demonstrate your determination and dedication during your next performance review! You can show that you are both people-oriented and results-oriented as you give a progress report on your meetings from one year to the next.

Within a day's time begin a **tentative agenda** for a follow-up meeting. List old business and new business before you forget or get sidetracked. Write **thank-you notes** to key contributors and helpful members. Begin periodic **check-in calls** to those members who are working on the action plan or on any other decisions made during the meeting and to those members who missed the meeting. Ask for **feedback** from friends who attended the meeting. **Evaluate** the group's performance, your performance, other leaders' performances and the overall production of the meeting. Set **personal goals** to achieve during the next meeting cycle. Give yourself credit for improving your leadership, communication and organization skills. In fact, use the **CReDiT** model on the next page to remind you of the tasks associated with finishing the agenda and evaluating the process.

The CReDiT Model

CReDiT

Critique: Decide what was good and what needs improvement.
Keep a journal.
Ask for feedback.
Evaluate.
Recognize: Follow up with your supporters.
Thank support staff in person.
Write thank-you notes.
Reward yourself.
Deliver: Follow through on your responsibilities.
Return property.
Keep promises.
Make check-in calls.
Begin next agenda.
Finish and distribute the minutes.
Transfer: Continue to learn and to improve your skills.
Network.
Set personal goals.
Review journal for insights.

Photocopy any of the evaluation models that follow on pages 152-155 or create your own. Use them regularly to monitor your meeting-planning development. They will help you keep your credibility rating high!

Presentation Evaluation

Whether you make out an evaluation for yourself or ask a co-worker to do it, keep a record of your progress as a meeting leader. The more specific your personal goals are for your presentation skills, the more likely you'll accomplish them. Video and audiotapes can record mannerisms you are unconscious of. Critique yourself regularly, so that others encounter fewer distractions in your meetings!

Public Speaking Evaluation

Most of your meetings require speaking with a group, but not to a group. Occasionally, though, you'll be asked to give presentations to the public. You're gaining a reputation as an organized planner with the meetings you're running. People are expecting you to represent your team to other groups. Use this form to keep a record of your efforts.

Group Processing Evaluation

Because groups vary from one meeting to another, keep track of the details and success of each group. Soon you'll see patterns that will give you insights about the people you work with and their communication styles. This information will tell you how to approach a given group the next time you meet!

Goal-Setting Worksheet

How do you know that you're developing the professional skills you need? One way is to manage yourself before your superior has a need to. Set your goals in clear, realistic statements. Leaders who are firm in their convictions and flexible in their communication continue to set goals and make opportunities for themselves. Now that you're conducting effective meetings, what else do you want to learn?

Presentation Evaluation

Task or Skill	Terrific (Strong)	Tenuous (So-so)	Terrible (Weak)
Elements:			
Greeting	_____	_____	_____
Opening	_____	_____	_____
Delivery	_____	_____	_____
Closing	_____	_____	_____
Feedback	_____	_____	_____
Preparation:			
Needs assessment	_____	_____	_____
Resources assessment	_____	_____	_____
Agenda	_____	_____	_____
Audience analysis	_____	_____	_____
Promotion	_____	_____	_____
Rehearsal	_____	_____	_____
Materials/visuals	_____	_____	_____
Appearance	_____	_____	_____
Training strategies	_____	_____	_____
Room arrangement	_____	_____	_____
Minutes	_____	_____	_____
Equipment	_____	_____	_____

Public Speaking Evaluation

Part I: Check the appropriate column for each item.

	Exc	Good	OK	Poor
Meeting date:_____				

Voice:

	Exc	Good	OK	Poor
Rate	[]	[]	[]	[]
Inflection	[]	[]	[]	[]
Volume	[]	[]	[]	[]

Diction:

	Exc	Good	OK	Poor
Correct pronunciation	[]	[]	[]	[]
Clear enunciation	[]	[]	[]	[]

	Exc	Good	OK	Poor
Gestures	[]	[]	[]	[]
Poise	[]	[]	[]	[]

Presentation:

	Exc	Good	OK	Poor
Content	[]	[]	[]	[]

Organization:

	Exc	Good	OK	Poor
Introduction/purpose	[]	[]	[]	[]
Body/logic	[]	[]	[]	[]
Conclusion/significance	[]	[]	[]	[]

Development:

	Exc	Good	OK	Poor
Analysis	[]	[]	[]	[]
Concrete, specific examples	[]	[]	[]	[]
Stories []	[]	[]	[]	

Part II:
Rate your overall performance and presentation._____

(Excellent, Good, OK, Poor)

153

Group Processing Evaluation

1. Was the group the appropriate size?

2. Did the room arrangement facilitate group participation?

3. Were there adequate breaks and movement between activities or agenda items?

4. Was the training strategy appropriate for the group?

5. Who were the discussion or task leaders?

6. Which participants acted withdrawn?

7. What could have been done to draw them out?

8. Which participants were dominant?

9. What could have been done to restrain them?

10. What conflicts or disagreements arose in the process?

11. How were the conflicts resolved or the disagreements transformed?

12. How could you improve the group dynamics in similar situations?

Goal-Setting Worksheet

1. What are your personal and professional goals?

2. What two or three objectives would support this goal?

   A.

   B.

   C.

3. What corporate vision, mission or objective statement is most closely related to your answers to the first two questions?

4. What is your specific plan of action and timetable?

   Step A: _____

      Completion date: _____

   Step B: _____

      Completion date: _____

   Step C: _____

      Completion date: _____

5. What are your realistic measurement criteria? How will you know when you have achieved your objectives and goal?

6. What is your target date? _____

7. When are your review dates? _____

Each one of the lists of tips, guidesheets and checklists included in this book is a potential evaluation form. Use the lists when organizing your meeting and again after the meeting is over. Complete the **Self-Assessment Survey** again and compare your answers. Congratulations! Celebrate your growth with affirmations.

Affirmations:

I am saving time by holding only necessary meetings.

I am saving time by starting and ending meetings at agreed times.

I am saving time by asking people to prepare or know background material prior to the meeting.

I am conserving effort by preparing essential materials before decision makers must act.

I am conserving effort by including all essential decision makers in the meeting.

I am saving time and effort by communicating better the first time.

I am saving time and effort by encouraging team collaboration.

I am saving money by using company resources as efficiently and effectively as possible.

I am learning new skills and improving current skills with each meeting.

I am organizing, communicating and leading better than ever before.

I am more aware, more confident, more competent, more visible and more assertive now than ever before and that feels good!

Sometimes it's impossible to know where one meeting ends and the next begins. Tying up all the loose ends of this meeting will help you determine if there is enough need to plan a follow-up meeting soon. A good meeting leader stays in contact with team members to maintain communication so that future meetings run smoothly. See how you're doing in this phase of your meeting planning.

Completion Checklist

Meeting Date:_____ **Meeting Objective:**_____

Task	Completed/Not Necessary
	(✗) (N/A)
Selected a closing	_____
Networked	_____
Thanked the support staff	_____
Thanked the contributors	_____
Returned property	_____
Rewarded myself	_____
Wrote in my journal	_____
Started the next agenda	_____
Distributed the minutes or summary memo	_____
Made check-in calls to absentees	_____
Made check-in calls to those involved in the action plan	_____
Asked for feedback	_____
Evaluated	_____
Set personal goals	_____

*I*NDEX

appeaser, 39
arbitrator, 114
assumptions, 108
Audience Analysis Worksheet, 43

B
behavioral catagories, 36
best ear, 108
Big, Bright, Bold, Bang Approach, 49
biographies, 125
body language, 111
    See also nonverbal
Brainstorm Spiral, 134-135
breathing, 118

C
card, 124
caregiver, 38
caretaker, 38
caring atmosphere in workplace, 48
catalysts, 36, 38
cautionary, 38
characteristics of groups, 86-88
chart:
    Meeting Summary Chart, 22
    Seating Arrangement Chart, 96
checklist:
    completion, 157
    preparation, 75
    presentation, 141
chevron style, 94, 97
circle style, 91, 97
classroom style, 93, 97
co-act, 104
collaborate, 104
colors, 72
commit, 147

160

T

U

V

values survey,   146
visionary,   38
visual displays,   59, 109, 119, 135-136
Visual Image Tips,   72
visualization,   74, 108
Vocal Image Tips,   73

W

Ways to Close a Meeting,   146-148
Ways to Increase Your Credibility,   137-139
Ways to Open a Meeting,   122-124
Ways to Reduce Anxiety,   118-120
Ways to Reduce Your Audience's Anxiety,   120-122
Ways to Reduce Your Own Anxiety,   118-120
worksheet:
 Agenda Planning Worksheet,   25-27
 Audience Analysis Worksheet,   43
 Needs Satisfaction Worksheet, 45
 "Role Call" Worksheet,   38, 39

Y

years,   123